Who Needs Theology? is a *cri de coeur*
from two of North America's leading theological
writers. Wide-ranging, impassioned and
eminently readable, this book should be required
reading for every student entering theological
study at whatever level.

But it is also a book to put into the hands of every
responsible pastor or layperson who seriously aspires
to embrace the biblical mandate to "love the Lord
our God with all of our mind."

In its own terms this is a prophetic writing whose
holistic vision of heart, mind and will united in the
service of God points a way back for evangelical
Christianity from the cultural margins toward the high
ground of cultural leadership and renewal.

BRUCE MILNE
Senior Minister
First Baptist Church, Vancouver

Grenz and Olson gently and persuasively
disarm the suspicions that many sincere believers bring
to the study of theology. They show that theology,
rightly practiced, is indispensable to Christian
living. At the same time they equip believers to begin
the journey of living "theologically."

JONATHAN WILSON
Westmont College

I found this book extremely helpful and
encouraging—a corrective to much confused "folk
theology" as well as a stimulus to do serious, reflective
thinking about God and his world. . . . A book for
pastors and thoughtful laymen, who are encouraged
to become maturing Christian thinkers.

ROGER FREDRIKSON
Former President
American Baptist Churches/USA

WHO NEEDS THEOLOGY?

An Invitation to the Study of God

Stanley J. Grenz & Roger E. Olson

InterVarsity Press
Downers Grove, Illinois, USA
Leicester, England

InterVarsity Press
P.O. Box 1400, Downers Grove, IL 60515, USA
38 De Montfort Street, Leicester LE1 7GP, England

InterVarsity Press®, U.S.A., is the book-publishing division of InterVarsity Christian Fellowship®, a student movement active on campus at hundreds of universities, colleges and schools of nursing in the United States of America, and a member movement of the International Fellowship of Evangelical Students. For information about local and regional activities, write Public Relations Dept., InterVarsity Christian Fellowship, 6400 Schroeder Rd., P.O. Box 7895, Madison, WI 53707-7895.

Inter-Varsity Press, England, is the book-publishing division of the Universities and Colleges Christian Fellowship (formerly the Inter-Varsity Fellowship), a student movement linking Christian Unions in universities and colleges throughout the United Kingdom and the Republic of Ireland, and a member movement of the International Fellowship of Evangelical Students. For information about local and national activities write to UCCF, 38 De Montfort Street, Leicester LE1 7GP.

UK ISBN 0-85111-177-7
USA ISBN 0-8308-1878-2

Printed in the United States of America ∞

Library of Congress Cataloging-in-Publication Data

Grenz, Stanley, 1950-
    Who needs theology?: an invitation to the study of God/by
Stanley J. Grenz and Roger E. Olson.
        p.   cm.
    Includes bibliographical references.
    ISBN 0-8308-1878-2 (paper: alk. paper)
    1. Theology—Introductions.   I. Olson, Roger E.   II. Title.
BT65.G75   1996
230'.01—dc20   *96-19405*
                                                          CIP

British Library Cataloguing in Publication Data

A catalogue record for this book is available from the British Library.

15	14	13	12	11	10	9	8	7	6	5	4	3	2	1
08	07	06	05	04	03	02	01	00	99	98	97	96		

Introduction

Many Christians today not only are uninformed about basic theology but even seem hostile to it. What has brought about this appalling lack of interest and frequently open hostility to theology among Christian laypeople, students and even pastors?

We are confident that this condition does not result from any inherent flaw in theology itself or in the intellectual or spiritual lives of ordinary Christians. Rather, it results from *popular and pervasive misunderstandings* of theology.

Both of us have taught theology in college or seminary settings for over a decade. During this time we have discovered among students a genuine hunger and thirst for deeper understanding of God and God's ways. We have both held numerous retreats, seminars and workshops for lay Christians and pastors and have found them open to serious study of and reflection on God's Word in the light of contemporary issues. But we have experienced a strange phenomenon: among those very people who are hungry for understanding and who may offer marvelous insights, a chill often descends as soon as the word *theology* is uttered.

A 1994 poll funded by the Murdock Charitable Trust and published in *Christianity Today* set out to discover churchgoers' priorities when seeking a pastor. Both laypeople and pastors rated "theological knowledge" last out of five qualifications most important for a good pastor.[1] At the same time, many professional theologians and ministers have been calling for a renewal of serious theological reflection by and among Christians. We agree that this is a laudable goal and, if attained, would enhance Christianity's credibility in a world that wants answers to life's ultimate questions.

Our decision to write this book arose out of our shared desire to see a revival of sound theological interest and reflection among God's people. We fear that Christianity may be in danger of becoming a mere "folk religion," relegated to realms of sheer subjectivity and emptied of public credibility, unless lay Christians and ministers catch the vision for an intellectually satisfying Christian belief system. We are also concerned that individual Christians who lack theological literacy and acumen will be tossed about by every wind of doctrine that comes sweeping through our media-dominated culture. From television preachers to spirituality sections of mainstream bookstores, all kinds of strange doctrines—"other gospels"—are being promoted and accepted by Christians unequipped to evaluate them.

We hope and pray that readers will catch a vision for sound theology through reading this book. We are not proposing that they become "professional theologians" as we are, or even that they agree with everything we have to say. Rather, we desire that they will become "salt and light" in a world that desperately needs bright, articulate Christians.

We have chosen to dedicate this book to a man we both admire and treasure. Dr. Ralph Powell taught systematic theology at North American Baptist Seminary in Sioux Falls, South Dakota, for over twenty-five years, and we were both influenced by his combination of deep spirituality and intellectual rigor. For me (Roger), Dr. Powell was the person who single-handedly stimulated real interest in theology. I will never forget the first day I heard Dr. Powell contradict a whining seminary student's complaint about our required reading of Emil

Brunner's *Dogmatics* with booming voice: "This is great stuff!" I agreed with him and grew to love him for his love of strong theological "stuff."

I (Stan) followed Dr. Powell as professor of theology at NABS upon his retirement. But it was not our first or only connection. Dr. Powell has been a lifelong friend, ever since my father became Ralph's pastor when I was two years old!

We proudly dedicate *Who Needs Theology?* to our pastor, teaching mentor and friend Dr. Ralph Powell.

1

Everyone Is
a Theologian

*A*n influential Christian Bible teacher and radio preacher once quipped, "Happy is the Christian who has never met a theologian!" What could he have meant? Misconceptions, stereotypes, myths and false impressions about theology abound—even within Christian communities. In fact, there seems to be a growing bias against theology and theologians in some Christian circles.

Every professional theologian knows and is frustrated by this prejudice against theology. One Sunday morning I (Roger) arrived to speak to an adult Sunday-school class on the topic "Twentieth-Century Theology" and was handed an anonymous letter addressed to me but sent to the church's address. The writer had seen an advertisement for the series of talks on the church page of the city's newspaper and had written out two pages of very intense objections to theology. Repeatedly the writer pitted prayer against theology and implied that theology is nothing but a poor substitute for a personal relationship with God!

Anonymous Theologians

The striking irony of the Bible teacher's aphorism and the letter-writer's diatribe is this: they are both theological in their own ways! *Theology* is any reflection on the ultimate questions of life that point toward God. Hence both the Bible teacher and the anonymous letter writer are theologians. We'll call them "anonymous theologians," because like most other people, they don't realize that's what they are.

No one who reflects on life's ultimate questions can escape theology. And anyone who reflects on life's ultimate questions—including questions about God and our relationship with God—is a theologian.

A young woman sat in my office sharing her dreams and aspirations. After taking a few courses in biblical and theological studies she had become intensely interested in exploring questions about God, salvation and Christian living. At a crucial turning point in the conversation she looked at me with some fear in her eyes and said, "You know, I think I'd like to be a theologian—if I can cut it!"

I detected that behind the fear was a misconception of *theologian* as an awesome creature who thinks deep and disturbing thoughts that very few people can understand. My response was meant to alleviate that anxiety. I said to her, "You already are a theologian!" I proceeded to explain that she might be called to make this aspect of her Christian existence—reflecting on life's ultimate questions, including God—a career, but whether she did or not was irrelevant to her being a theologian.

A misconception is growing among Christians that a great gulf exists between "ordinary Christians" and "theologians." For some that perceived gap creates fear; for others it creates suspicion and resentment. We want to close the gap by showing that everyone—especially every Christian—is a theologian and that every professional theologian is simply a Christian whose vocation is to do what all Christians do in some way: think and teach about God.

Throughout this book, then, we will be attempting to show two things: First, theology is inescapable for all thinking, reflecting Christians, and the difference between lay theologians and professional theologians is one of degree, not kind. Second, professional theologians and lay theologians (all reflective Christians of whatever profession) need one another. Professional theologians exist to serve the community of faith, not to dictate to it or lord over it intellectually. Lay theologians need professional theologians to give them the tools of biblical study, historical perspective and systematic articulation so that they can improve their own theologizing.

Theology comes from a combination of two Greek words: *theos,* which means "God," and *logos,* which means "reason," "wisdom" or "thought." Literally, then, *theology* means "God-thought" or "reasoning about God." Some dictionaries define it more formally and specifically as "the science of God," but *science* in this sense simply means "reflection on something." So at its most basic level *theology* is any thinking, reflecting or contemplating on the reality of God—even on the question of God.

The question of God is implied in all of life's ultimate questions. Whenever and wherever a person reflects on the great "Why?" questions of life, at least indirect reflection on or toward God is involved. God is the horizon of all human wondering. This means that in amazing ways even popular authors, composers, playwrights, poets and creators of pop culture function as theologians.

One outstanding example is famous filmmaker and actor Woody Allen. Some of Allen's films focus on psychology, but many of them deal with theology as well. In *Crimes and Misdemeanors* Allen explores the great question asked repeatedly by the Old Testament psalmist: "Why do the wicked prosper and the righteous suffer?" While the explicit question of God may not arise often in this film, the theme of God is implicit within and beneath the agonizing question of "Why?" Why? Because, of course, if there is no God, then this is not an agonizing question at all! Why agonize over what may simply be a natural law—the so-called survival of the fittest? "Why do the wicked prosper and the righteous suffer?" is an agonizing question only if God is the ultimate horizon of human existence. Then the question is ultimately a question about God: "Why does God allow such things to happen?" Woody Allen and other anonymous theologians of popular culture raise this question in surprising and often very helpful ways.

Worldviewish Theology

Every person must at some point in life face and wrestle with the questions that point to the ultimate question of God. Many people, admittedly, do not formulate the question of God explicitly. Nevertheless, even where God is ignored or denied, God remains the ultimate horizon—background and goal—against which all of life's ultimate questions arise and to which they point. In this sense every thinking person is a theologian.

One way to begin grasping the universality of theology, then, is to see it as wondering and thinking about life's ultimate questions. Wheaton College philosophy professor Arthur Holmes has labeled this most basic and universal kind of theologizing "worldviewish theology." That is, from time immemorial ordinary people, men and women in the street and in the marketplace, as well as professional thinkers in their ivory towers, have pondered certain perennial questions of life.

In our less reflective moments perhaps many of us think some of these questions sound silly. For example, one modern philosopher has argued that the most basic question of all is "Why is there something rather than nothing?" Yet even this seemingly abstract and unanswerable question has a certain pull to it, for it is simply a larger expression of the more common question every thinking person asks once in a while: "Why am I here?" Other ultimate questions of life include "What am I to do with my existence?" "What is the truly 'good life'?" and "Is there anything after death?"

The ultimate question of all life's ultimate questions is the question of God, for this is the question to which all others point. If God—the "maker of heaven and earth"—exists, then all other questions take on new significance and receive possible answers where otherwise they seem only to lead into dead ends.

Worldviewish theology is common to every thinking person, for wondering about life's ultimate questions constitutes part of our human existence. That in itself may be a significant pointer toward Someone beyond ourselves.

Christian Theology

But what about Christian theology? Doesn't that go beyond theology in the vague, all-inclusive sense described above? Indeed it does. What might be a proper basic definition of Christian theology, then? One time-honored definition is "faith seeking understanding." In spite of misconceptions to the contrary, Christian theology does not say "understand and then believe." Rather, theology is seeking to understand with the intellect what the heart—a person's central core of character—already believes and to which it is committed.

This definition of theology goes back at least to the great medieval theologian Anselm of Canterbury. Anselm was a monk, philosopher-theologian and archbishop of Canterbury during the twelfth century. He is famous for formulating what is supposed by many to be the perfect rational proof for the existence of God—the so-called ontological proof, in which he purported to demonstrate beyond any possible doubt that God must exist from the definition of God as "the being greater than which none can be conceived."

Because of his writings, Anselm has gained the undeserved reputation of being a hard-core rationalist—one who refuses to believe anything that cannot be proved. In fact, however, Anselm wrote most of his great works, including his versions of the ontological argument for God's existence, in the form of prayers! In one such prayer he made it absolutely clear that he was not attempting to prove God's existence in order to believe but because he already believed. His motto was "Credo ut intelligam"—"I believe in order that I may understand."

Faith seeking understanding, then, is another way of stating Anselm's approach to theology. One begins with faith as ultimately a mysterious gift of grace, which, however, does not mean the person has no role in having it. But faith is more than simply choosing to believe something, and it is certainly more than a poor substitute for having good reasons. Faith is being grasped by someone—Someone!—who calls and claims one's life.

This is how the Christian life begins—with grace and faith, not reason. Reason may play a role and be an instrument in God's call, but one never becomes a Christian simply by reaching the end of a purely human chain of reasoning and concluding, "Well, I guess if I want to be reasonable I have to believe in God and Jesus Christ." No, the genesis of authentic Christianity may include a process of reasoning, but it cannot be reduced to that. Faith is that mysterious element which involves personal conviction, an insight from somewhere else, a transformation of heart that inclines one toward God in a new way.

Connecting Worldviewish and Christian Theologies

How shall we connect these two types of theology—the one common to all thinking persons (worldviewish theology) and the other common to all Christians? It seems that life's ultimate questions serve as signals or clues of transcendence; that is, they point upward to something or someone beyond finite, creaturely existence. We may call this process and practice of reflecting on life's ultimate questions "humanity's search for God." It is a universal search that seems always to be frustrated *unless* the search turns around and becomes "God's search for humankind."

That is exactly what Christians believe happened in the history the Bible narrates. God began sending answers to the human search through historical events, through groups of people and their prophets, through inspired messages, and ultimately through God's own coming in person to be with and among humans. Christians believe that this history and its narrative in the Bible provide the answers to life's ultimate questions. But receiving them and recognizing them as God's Word to humans is a work of God's grace and a result of faith. In the end, acknowledging God is not merely a philosophical discovery, although a person may first become open to God and God's Word through recognizing this connection between the answers found there and life's ultimate and perennial questions.

So Christian theology goes beyond worldviewish theology by completing and fulfilling it. Every Christian, then, is not only a theologian in the Woody Allen sense of reflecting on life's ultimate questions, but is also a Christian theologian in that he or she reflects on the meaning of God's Word and how it illumines life, giving meaning and purpose to existence.

Authentic Christian faith always inclines one toward understanding the God who has claimed our lives. And to the extent that a Christian seeks to understand the meaning of faith for answering life's ultimate questions or for simply answering basic questions about growing in relation to God, he or she is already a theologian.

You, then, are a Christian theologian. You may never have thought of yourself that way. And perhaps you have always thought of theology as something mysterious or even dangerous. Many Christians falsely equate theology with questioning God or questioning the authority of the Bible and then conclude that theology is a threat to faith. Perhaps you have labored under these misconceptions or know someone who has. Perhaps you have been warned by some well-meaning Christian to beware of the study of theology because it might destroy your faith.

We have experienced that discouraging warning from family and friends. Some of our spiritual mentors have tried to dissuade us from the study of theology because of the deeply ingrained bias that sees it as a substitute for faith. We are glad that we overcame those objections, because for us theology has been and is a liberating and enriching study that constantly brings us closer to God.

Levels of Theology in Practice

So far we have said that everyone is a theologian and that every

Christian is or should be a Christian theologian. The ways in which we have defined *theology, theologian* and *Christian theologian* may seem to stack the cards in favor of our argument. We have not been playing word tricks; rather we have been trying to show that there are distinct levels of theology. All Christians may be theologians, but not all theologies are thereby made equal. We will explore the distinct types and levels of theology in the next chapter, but for now some anticipation of that discussion is in order.

To help elucidate the claim that everyone is a theologian, we will use some analogies. Would you buy it if we said that everyone is a chemist? a political scientist? a psychologist? a mathematician? Anyone who cooks using recipes is a chemist in some sense. Without a rudimentary—at least intuitive—knowledge of substances, measures, combinations and effects of temperatures, one could never cook anything.

Cooking, then, is perhaps the most basic form of lay chemistry. But suppose an amateur cook decides to improve his skills in order to please guests' palates with culinary delights. The safest and surest path is to take a course and read a few books. A cook becomes a chef by developing his knowledge and skills of chemistry. Of course this is still a far cry from the science of chemistry as studied and practiced in university laboratories! Nevertheless, there is a certain continuity between the chef's practice of culinary arts and the chemist's science.

Anyone who participates in a town meeting, school-board session or political party caucus is a political scientist. Suppose the untutored voter decides to become a school-board candidate. In the process she will necessarily sharpen and fine-tune her knowledge of and ability to practice political science. She may read a few good books on political theory and develop a philosophy of the "polis" (community) out of that. Of course this is a far cry from the highly theoretical and sometimes speculative discipline of political science itself as taught in universities. Nevertheless, there is a real continuity between the informed participant's involvement in party politics and the political scientist's theorizing.

The same analogies can be drawn within the spheres of psychology and mathematics. In some way every person is an amateur psychologist. But whenever a person chooses to go beyond intuitive dream interpretation and explore the workings of the subconscious mind, he moves toward the science of psychology. Balancing a checkbook is a rudimentary form of mathematics, yet there are, of course, much deeper waters of the subject to wade in if one chooses to.

Suppose you overheard an amateur cook complaining about the formal science of chemistry because it cannot be exhaustively practiced in the kitchen but requires specialized tools, vocabulary and concepts that one usually finds only in well-equipped laboratories and libraries. "Happy is the cook who has never met a chemist!" Absurd? Of course.

Suppose you overheard a delegate at a neighborhood political caucus complaining about political scientists because their theories are difficult to understand and "take the life out of" politics. Suppose the lay student of dreams complained because psychologists are so intellectual, or suppose the bank teller whined that mathematics is so abstract. All of these absurdities could happen—and perhaps do! But most people would raise an eyebrow and say something like "You know, you might be a better cook if you knew a little more about chemistry and equipped your kitchen a little better," or "Handling money might be more fun than mathematics, but without the latter you could be shortchanging customers or the bank."

Our point should be obvious: because Christians are people who believe in God and also believe that God relates to them in special ways (through God's Word, grace, faith, prayer and so on), they would do well to explore the meaning of God and try to get to know God as thoroughly as possible with their whole being—mind as well as heart. They should recognize themselves as lay theologians and appreciate the help they might receive from more formal, professional theology. Of course, as professional theologians, we acknowledge that the very reason for our profession lies in aiding lay Christians and pastors to enhance their understanding of God. Continuity and correspondence should replace hostility, fear or suspicion between lay and professional theologians. In discovering truth about God and God's relation to us, they are interdependent and mutually beneficial to one another.

The title of our book is *Who Needs Theology?* The answer we develop throughout is similar to what might appear in a similar book entitled *Who Needs Chemistry?* aimed at cooks and housekeepers. One can imagine another book entitled *Who Needs Psychology?* aimed at people who seek self-understanding. *Who Needs Mathematics?* might be a good book for people who balance ledgers, do taxes or compute grades! The answers to all these title questions would be the same—*everyone does!* Each book would probably make the point that every reader is already a chemist or psychologist or mathematician—on some level. Readers would probably respond quite enthusiastically to those messages.

We hope that you will respond enthusiastically to the message that you are already a theologian—even if it comes as quite a shock. Of course we do not mean that you are already or ever will be a professional theologian—not everyone should be. But we hope that once you see that you are a theologian, you will resist messages from even pious Christians who try to tell you that theology is something bad or just a "head trip" or a threat to true faith. It does not have to be, and at its best it never is.

But now we've gone from talking about theology in the most general sense to theology "at its best." What does it mean to talk about different types and levels of theology and to contend that not all theologies are equal? Those are the questions to which we now turn.

2

Not All Theologies
Are Equal

*P*eanuts character Linus, always inclined toward theological reflection, stands next to his bed, examining his hands clasped as in prayer. As his sister Lucy approaches, he announces, "I think I've made a new theological discovery."

Lucy asks curiously, "What is it?" as Linus continues to study his hands.

To her obvious dismay, he replies sincerely, "If you hold your hands upside down, you get the opposite of what you pray for!"

An earnest young university student sat across the desk from me (Roger), sputtering protests against my critical evaluation of his theology essay. "I worked hard on this and studied the Bible in more detail on this subject than anyone has! In fact, I've been studying what the Bible says about this for several years—ever since an evangelist preached on it at camp when I was in high school. How can you cut down my paper like this?"

I had given him a passing grade—but not the one he had hoped for and expected. While I keenly felt his disappointment and sympathized with him, I could not help feeling frustrated at his lack of understanding of theology at the end of two semesters in my courses.

The student, like many Christians, believed that all theology consists of (or *should* consist of) is detailed study of the Bible, comparing and contrasting passages in a sort of commonsense way. His paper was a twenty-page magnum opus on his favorite subject—the apostle Paul's understanding of human nature. Terms like *body, soul, spirit, heart* and *flesh* were his bread and butter. But unfortunately he had consciously rejected my pleas and urgings to study these terms using commentaries, books of word studies that would explain the subtle nuances of their meanings in the original languages, and sources that would elucidate the cultural and religious background against which Paul used these terms. Instead the student had simply relied on individual intuition as he read the English translation his home church favored. He was almost totally unaware of the deeply ingrained presuppositions that he brought to the texts as he studied them, and he rejected any notion that these terms might not mean what they seemed on the surface to mean—*to him.*

Frankly, the paper was a mess. Ignoring hundreds of years of careful study of Paul's theology, it attempted to jump directly over all of that right back into Paul's head (or the Holy Spirit's mind!), using intuition and a poor English translation of Paul's Greek writings. The result was an account of Paul's anthropology that was nearly completely wrong. Like many who attempt to interpret Paul's terms without any scholarly help, the student equated "body" and "flesh" and thus ended up with an anthropology nearly identical to that of Paul's opponents in the early church!

In the final analysis the student let his true feelings show toward me, the dreaded professional theologian and Bible scholar: "Who are *you* to say my interpretation of Paul's theology of the human person is wrong? *My* Bible is plain and simple, and all you scholars do is complicate it and make it impossible for ordinary people to understand. Well, I prefer my commonsense approach to your scholastic one." With that final protest the student stomped out of my office, and I never saw him again.

Who needs theology? Anyone who is already engaged in a particular study and practicing a discipline needs to reflect on it ever more deeply. So you—like everyone else—need theology, because, insofar as you are a thinking person who at least occasionally reflects on life's ultimate questions and a Christian who seeks to understand and apply God's Word, you are doing theology. Theology is not, as many wrongly suppose, a kind of esoteric knowledge possessed by a few superior intellectuals. It is simply *faith seeking understanding.* And insofar as ordinary Christians seek answers to questions that naturally arise out of faith, they are already doing Christian theology.

We are well aware, however, that many perceptive readers may agree with our point so far and yet have serious reservations about the need for or value of formal, professional theology and theologians. If every Christian is already a theologian and is doing theology, why have professional theologians? And don't professional theologians— those who specialize in this study and get paid for researching and teaching—complicate beyond all comprehension the simple faith that ordinary Christians seek to understand?

We will deal with these and other common objections to formal, professional theology later in the book. For now, we acknowledge this problem. It is not enough simply to point out that all Christians are already theologians when there are so many different types and levels of theology. Many Christians who object to theology mean by that term something quite different from ordinary, simple reflection on their Christian faith.

Implicit in this objection is what we will call a *populist mentality* toward Christianity and theology. *Populist* means "of the people." It is a term often used in politics to designate very negative attitudes toward professional politicians and those in power. In theology it may mean a negative attitude toward those who have specialized knowledge and expertise in understanding the Christian faith. The populist mindset says, "Why can't all theologies be equal? Who needs professional theology and theologians? If all ordinary Christians are theologians, why are people with doctorates writing volumes and volumes of formal theological works and teaching a discipline that we all already know so much about?"

You probably knew when you picked up this book that the title—*Who Needs Theology?*—really means "Who needs something more formal, reflective and systematic than ordinary lay theology such as all Christians engage in?" But before we proceed throughout the rest of the volume to explain and defend formal, reflective theology, we need to expound as many different levels of theology as we can. There are many different layers or levels of theologizing. Some are good and helpful, whereas others are dangerous.

Reflective Christianity

Types of theologizing can be seen as lying along a spectrum of reflection. By *reflection* we mean formalized thinking—using our minds to organize our thoughts and beliefs, bring them into coherence with one another by attempting to identify and expunge blatant contradictions, and make sure that there are good reasons for interpreting Christian faith in the way we do. Reflection, then, involves a certain amount of critical thinking—questioning the ways we think and why we believe and behave the way we do. It usually involves the use of logic (however rudimentary) and some historical consciousness (awareness of historical sources and development of ideas) as well as some amount of objectivity toward one's own assumed beliefs and life practices.

Some readers may be thinking, *Why should reflection be a part of Christianity? Aren't Christians supposed to believe like children and simply accept by blind faith what has been given to them by God's Word?* Earlier we defined theology as faith seeking understanding. By reflection we mean the seeking with the mind that begins with a certitude about God and God's Word and attempts to discover what truly is implied there about believing and living. It does include a recognition of the possibility that we may have been believing wrongly or incompletely. God or God's Word is not wrong, but our human attempts to interpret and apply God's Word may have been wrong. Reflection is a necessary part of any maturing thought process.

The ancient Athenian philosopher Socrates held the motto "The unexamined life is not worth living." By "unexamined life" he meant unreflective living—living moment-to-moment without thinking critically about what one believes and how one behaves. We hold that in a sense "the unexamined (unreflective) faith is not worth believing." In other words, part of the process of maturing in Christian faith is examining—reflecting critically on—one's own and others' beliefs and lifestyles. But that does not mean laying aside all faith-commitments in the process. One never reflects in a vacuum! It may simply mean sitting back or going into the library and examining one's secondary values and behaviors in the light of one's core beliefs and values. "Are they consistent? Is there a wholeness—an integrity—to what I believe and how I live my life?" This is the beginning of a reflective faith.

Theologies, then, lie along a spectrum of reflection. At one extreme end is what we will call "folk theology," while at the other end lies its opposite, "academic theology." Between these lie various levels of theology—some less and some more reflective in their approaches to understanding Christian faith. Closer to the center of the spectrum than folk theology is lay theology, and closer yet is ministerial theology. Moving on toward the other end of the spectrum we find professional theology, and finally—at the opposite extremity from folk theology—lies academic theology:

| ← | folk theology | lay theology | ministerial theology | professional theology | academic theology | → |

Folk Theology

What is folk theology? We will use the term to describe unreflective believing based on blind faith in a tradition of some kind. We are not using this label to criticize the simple faith of saints of God who have never been tutored in formal theology. We know some genuine saints who have lived out the Christian life in profound ways yet are not very good at articulating or critically reflecting on their beliefs. Rather, we use the term *folk theology* to refer to a kind of theology that rejects critical reflection and enthusiastically embraces simplistic acceptance of an informal tradition of beliefs and practices composed mainly of clichés and legends.

Folk theology is found in every denomination and very commonly among people who consider themselves Christians (or at least believers in God) but have no denominational or church affiliation. For the most part, folk theology completely rejects reflection in the sphere of religion. Deep spiritual piety and intellectual reflection are considered antithetical to one another within folk theology.

Most Christians engaged in folk theology would never consider it "theology." But in our broad sense of the term it is theology nevertheless, because it contains answers to life's ultimate questions and seeks to provide some kind of framework for believing and living the Christian faith. Folk theology is often intensely experiential and pragmatic—that is, the criteria of true belief are feelings and results. It is epitomized and perpetuated by various popular Christian bumper stickers, choruses, clichés and legends.

During the 1950s a popular Christian song carried the message "If I am dreaming, let me dream on!" The author, a devout Christian, had been told by a skeptic that his faith was nothing more than a pipe dream. His response was in the title of the song. In the 1960s, when some so-called Christian theologians were proclaiming the "death of God," a popular bumper sticker appeared that stated, "My God's not dead; sorry about yours!"

During the 1970s and 1980s many young Christians began to use the phrase "Our God is an awesome God!" to sum up their belief, and many Christians began watching television evangelists instead of attending church. The television evangelists and their guests often told sensational stories with little substance and no evidence. Yet these "accounts" caught on and spread like wildfire through their scattered congregations. One such "evangelegend" reported the discovery of hell by Russian scientists trying to dig a hole into the heart of the earth. Other evangelegends that provided "support" for Christian belief and on which many Christians hung their faith had to do with the Bermuda Triangle, hitchhiking angels, and astronomers who discovered Joshua's missing day by constructing sophisticated computer models.

The chief characteristic of folk theology is its attachment of unquestioning belief to these highly informal, unsubstantiated oral traditions and its refusal to measure them by any kind of warrants (grounds for believing). They are simply believed because they sound spiritual, or are delivered by a spiritual person, or convey a spiritual feeling. Any attempt to examine them objectively is eschewed and often even criticized as unspiritual.

One contemporary example of folk theology is the upsurge of interest in angels. Walk into any bookstore—secular or religious—and you will find scores of books about angels and other supernatural spiritual beings. Often the basis of what is written is pure folk theology—unverifiable stories of encounters with angels that lead to conclusions about the capabilities of angels. Some of these books even encourage readers to make contact with "your own inner angel."

Folk theology is evident when people adopt what is reported and advocated in such books (or television programs, sermons, audiotapes, videos and so on) for no better reason than that it sounds spiritual or gives comfort, and then resist any corrective or cautionary comments with something to the effect of "Don't confuse me with any facts; my mind is already made up." Folk theology, then, is unreflective belief that revels in subjective feelings brought on by slogans or legends and that resists examination. Generally speaking, it is quite comfortable with inner inconsistency and unquestioning belief in sensational stories and pithy clichés, which are the primary media for its communication.

Folk theology is inadequate as a resting place for most Christians. It encourages gullibility, vicarious spirituality and simplistic answers to difficult dilemmas that arise from being followers of Jesus Christ in a largely secular and pagan world. It stunts growth and blunts the influence of Christianity in the world. Further, it is often difficult to distinguish Christian folk theology from the canned answers and pasted smiles that cultists display on the doorstep as they peddle their "new revelations" from door to door.

Can folk theology be of value to reflective Christian faith? Might lay and professional theologians look to it as a resource? While folk theology is not adequate as a plateau for most Christians seeking to reflect on and articulate their beliefs, we do acknowledge that lay, ministerial and professional theologians can learn about the yearnings of people's hearts from studying it. The legends and clichés on which folk theology thrives reveal the spiritual needs, questions and desires of the masses. These should not be ignored, but rather drawn upon to show the resources of reflective faith for meeting and answering them.

Lay Theology
Lay theology is a step above and beyond folk theology in its level of reflection. In fact, given that reflection defines the difference between folk theology and lay theology, the latter may better be described as a quantum leap beyond the former! Lay theology appears when ordinary Christians begin to question folk theology with its childish, simplistic clichés and legends. It arises when Christians dig deeply into the resources of their faith, putting mind and heart together in a serious attempt to examine and understand that faith. Lay theology may lack sophisticated tools of biblical languages, logic and historical consciousness, but it seeks with what means it has to bring Christian

beliefs into a well-founded, coherent whole by questioning unfounded traditions and expunging blatant contradictions.

An example of lay theology happened in church when a Christian layman began to think about the words being sung in worship. He noticed that the worship leader chose hymns and choruses that seemed to contradict one another as well as the sermons the pastor was preaching. On Missions Sunday the guest preacher delivered a rousing sermon on the imminent coming of Jesus Christ and the need to evangelize the world to prepare for his arrival. The picture of the immediate future the evangelist portrayed was dismal—a world increasing in darkness, sin and error. Then Christ would appear to defeat the enemies of his kingdom and to begin his glorious thousand-year reign with his saints on earth!

The layman recognized this as the view generally held by the entire congregation and its denomination, and he even knew the theological term for it—*premillennialism.* Immediately after the sermon the worship leader invited the congregation to stand and sing as its closing hymn "We've a Story to Tell to the Nations." For the first time the layman reflected on the words in light of the sermon and recognized a serious inconsistency. The song implies that the millennial kingdom of Christ will come gradually through evangelism and social action: ". . . and the darkness shall turn to dawning and the dawning to noonday bright, and Christ's great kingdom shall come to earth, a kingdom of love and light." *This is* post*millennialism,* the lay theologian thought to himself.

The reflective Christian layman approached a member of the pastoral staff after the service and politely asked if he had noticed the discrepancy. He was rebuffed with a reply that insulted such examination as ruining the "spirit of worship"—folk theology!

The church needs more lay theologians like the man in this story! Such thinking Christians can help the church "get its act together" and present a face to itself and to the world that is consistent, knowing what it believes and why it believes what it proclaims. Unfortunately, however, even unsophisticated, polite lay theology is treated as evidence of diminishing spirituality by those who prefer folk theology. This reaction discourages and intimidates many lay Christians who want a more examined and reasonable faith. And it gives the impression that Christians in general are anti-intellectual and prefer comfortable myths to reasonable faith.

Ministerial Theology

Ministerial theology is reflective faith as practiced by trained ministers and teachers in Christian churches. It rises above lay theology in the level of reflection it involves. Ministerial theology is not only for ordained ministers or church professionals; the need in church life for lay people to minister through teaching, preaching, exhorting and evangelism is great. Sensing this need, many churches establish informal training centers to move reflective lay Christians toward semiprofessional ministerial theology. In addition, many lay Christians attend Bible colleges or evening seminary classes or take correspondence courses to enrich their ability to interpret Scripture and apply it to everyday life in an increasingly post-Christian world.

Ministerial theology at its best uses tools ordinarily available only through some kind of formal course work—a working knowledge of biblical languages or at least an ability to use concordances, commentaries and other printed helps; a historical perspective on the developments in theology through the ages; and keen systematic thinking that involves recognizing inconsistencies among beliefs and bringing beliefs into coherence with one another. Ministerial theology, then, is theology that stands somewhere between the beginning-level reflectiveness of the maturing lay Christian thinker and the more sophisticated and sustained reflectiveness of the professional theologian.

Professional Theology

Professional theology is further along the spectrum of reflection and professional preparation. The professional theologian is a person whose vocation involves studying the tools mentioned in the previous paragraph and instructing lay people and pastors in their use. Naturally enough, professional theologians attempt to raise their students above folk theology by inculcating in them a critical consciousness that questions unfounded assumptions and beliefs. To do this, professional theologians must themselves have a critical consciousness. This sometimes appears to others as skepticism and hostility toward piety and devotion. Professional theologians labor under this perception—often with great agony.

Together we (Stan and Roger) walked into the faculty lounge of a leading Christian liberal arts college to conduct a dialogue about integration of faith and learning with teachers of many different disciplines. No sooner had we sat down and eased into the conversation than one faculty member recounted a parable he had heard about theologians. According to the parable, a poor, benighted Christian was wandering around in a darkening forest trying to find his way out with one little candle to guide him. Suddenly a theologian came along and blew it out. Of course, in the parable, the candle represents folk theology and the candle snuffer is a professional theologian!

We would alter the parable. A man was wandering around in the darkening forest. Unfortunately, the poor man was simply going in circles because he was using a dim flashlight to see the way. But then a theologian came along, provided new batteries for his flashlight and pointed him in the direction out of the forest. In order to help the ever-circling man, the theologian had to criticize the dying batteries!

Professional theologians often have the feeling that some Christians have so much invested in their folk theology that they would rather no one pointed out to them that such theology is useless for answering the difficult questions posed for Christian faith in an ever-darkening world. While professional theologians may not be able to help persons who insist on living the Christian life by means of the meager help of folk theology, their main task and contribution lies in serving lay theologians and ministers. Professional theologians teach pastors in seminaries or church-related colleges and universities, and they write books and articles to aid lay and ministerial theologians in their journeys of reflection. At its best, professional theology functions in a *servant role* and not a *lordly role*. That is, the professional theologian serves the Christian community by helping people think like Christ so that they can be more effective in witness, work, and service both in the church and in the world.

Academic Theology

At the far end of the spectrum—beyond professional theology and completely opposite folk theology—is academic theology. This is a highly speculative, virtually philosophical theology aimed primarily at other theologians. It is often disconnected from the church and has little to do with concrete Christian living.

Professional theologians may sometimes benefit from the study of academic theology, and they usually are required to study it to some extent to earn their degrees, yet the church and individual Christians struggling in the real world gain little from it. While academic theologians are extremely reflective, they may take this good thing too far—cutting reflection off from faith and seeking understanding for its own sake. At its worst, academic theology follows the motto "I will believe only what I can understand," which is quite different from "faith seeking understanding."

Contemporary novelist John Updike has written an entire novel about the conflicts between some of the types of theology described above. The main character of *Roger's Version*[1] is Roger Lambert, a middle-aged professor of historical theology at a university divinity school in New England. He is the epitome of the academic theologian who seems more interested in his thoughts about God than in God himself! Early in the story he encounters a serious young folk theologian—a student of computer science at the university—who wants to prove that God exists by means of computer models and is completely uninterested in formal, academic theology. Their encounters and interactions provide an interesting—but not necessarily edifying!—case study in extremes along the spectrum of theological reflection. Much antipathy to theology arises from people's misperception that these are the only two types of theology—one that is impervious to critical thinking, often demonizing reflection as the sin of doubt, and another that is haughty and aloof, often contemptuous of ordinary Christians' questions and concerns.

Interdependent Theologies

Folk theology and academic theology are of little value—except when one is writing a narrative full of tension and conflict set in a university divinity school. In fact, they may at times be dangerous to the task of examining, understanding and articulating Christian faith. The types of theology lying between these are all necessary and beneficial, and they actually interpenetrate one another. Ministerial theologians are to use the tools and methods of professional theologians to instruct and enrich lay theologians in being prepared to give an answer to everyone who asks the reason for their hope (1 Pet 3:15).

Who needs theology? The Christian church and individual Christians who seek to grow in their faith need lay, ministerial and professional theology. Of course not every individual Christian needs to become a professional theologian. However, lay Christians who seek to increase the understanding of their faith and rise above folk theology need the help of ministerial theologians who in turn use the tools, training and insights of professional theologians. Professional theologians need the community of lay Christians led by pastors as their context for thought and critical reflection. Their purpose is to serve that community—even when their service is not entirely understood or appreciated.

So when we say that "not all theologies are equal," we do not mean that professional theology is better than ministerial theology or that ministerial theology is better than lay theology. What we do mean is that those three are preferable to folk theology. And among themselves they are equally valuable even though they involve different levels of skill in reflection on Christian faith and its meaning. These three levels of theology need each other, and the lines of communication and ties among them need strengthening. Without ministerial and professional theology, lay theology all too easily tends to slide backward into folk theology. The young university student in the example at the beginning of this chapter was a lay theologian who was sliding into folk theology because of his refusal to accept correction and help from professional theology.

The character in *Roger's Version* became an academic theologian, in part at least by slowly sliding into contempt for the church and for "ordinary" Christians and by valuing his own thoughts about God more than he valued the community of God's people, whose servant he should have been. This is the all-too-common fate of professional theologians who do not have regular contact with lay Christians and their pastors.

In chapter three we will provide a more formal definition and description of theology. Then we will proceed to defend it against some of the common objections thoughtful people raise against it, explain its tasks and traditions, and point out how every Christian can begin to do lay theology and experience the enrichment it can bring.

3

Defining Theology

*C*harlie Brown sits in front of Lucy's "Psychiatric Help" booth as the "doctor" waxes eloquent: "Life, Charlie Brown, is like a deck chair."

"Like a what?" he exclaims.

Lucy explains: "Have you ever been on a cruise ship? Passengers open up these canvas deck chairs so they can sit in the sun." Pointing to her left, she continued, "Some people place their chairs facing the rear of the ship so they can see where they've been." Then gesturing in the opposite direction, she says, "Other people face their chairs forward. They want to see where they're going!"

The explanation completed, Lucy turns to the "patient" sitting on the stool and demands, "On the cruise ship of life, Charlie Brown, which way is your deck chair facing?"

The boy thinks for a moment and then replies, "I've never been able to get one unfolded."

Whenever people give serious reflection to the ultimate questions of life, such as which way their deck chair is facing, they are engaging in theology. Viewed in this sense, everyone—Lucy, Charlie Brown, you, I, each of our friends and neighbors—is a theologian. Why is this the case? Why do the deepest questions of humankind lead to theology? Because in the end life's ultimate questions move beyond life. As we've noted already, these questions center around the question of God.

People find themselves in the realm of theology whenever they raise questions of ultimacy. Sometimes, however, their questions are more overtly and self-consciously theological. You have undoubtedly asked at one point or another: Is there really a God? What is God like? Or, Why does God allow evil? Each of these is a *theological* question. Theology explores general questions such as these.

Theology doesn't remain on the purely general level, however. Each person has at one time or another asked: Is God concerned about *me?* Does God love *me?* Or, How can *I* find God? These highly personal questions also lie in the domain of theology.

Theology seeks answers to general and personal questions about God, ultimate meaning, purpose and truth. But this way of defining theology is only partial, and because of its generality, it is wholly inadequate for describing the discipline (the science or formal study) of theology. Therefore, let us define it more precisely.

What Is Theology?
When confronted with a new term, it is often helpful to go first to the dictionary in order to understand it. Consider this simple, straightforward dictionary definition: Theology is "the study of God, his attributes, and his relationship with man and the universe."[1]

A first reaction upon reading this may well be, "The dictionary makes theology sound so sterile. Can that be what theology is all about?" Despite its seeming sterility, the dictionary definition does encapsule a central dimension of theology. As we explained in chapter one, the English word comes from two Greek terms, *theos* ("God") and *logos* ("word," "teaching," "study"). Viewed from this perspective, theology means "the teaching concerning God" or "the study of God." This is surprisingly similar to the dictionary definition.

In the broad sense theology is the attempt to reach below the surface of life and gain a deeper understanding of God. Theology seeks to understand God's being, God's nature and God's relationship to the world. It answers questions such as: What is God like? How does God treat us? What does God do? And it poses queries like: Is *everything* God? Or is God distinct from the universe and its processes?

As the quest to gain an understanding of God, theology is an ancient and respected intellectual discipline. For centuries philosophers have groped after answers to questions about the existence and nature of whatever supreme being there may be. And religious teachers have always sought to understand, describe and explain God.

In this general sense, theology is not uniquely Christian. It is rather a nearly universal human endeavor, of which Christian theology is a specific embodiment. The unique thing about Christian theology is that Christians seek answers to the ultimate questions by looking to Jesus Christ because they are convinced that "Jesus is the answer." That is, Christians believe that Jesus has revealed truth and ultimacy to us because he is the revelation of the very heart of God. Since Christian theology explores the beliefs about God and the world that are uniquely Christian by looking to Jesus, we may say that *Christian theology is reflecting on and articulating the beliefs about God and the world that Christians share as followers of Jesus Christ.*

Theology seeks to discover answers to ultimate questions by exploring the uniquely Christian belief system. It looks at the Christian way of understanding life, the world and all reality. Christians who study and write about theology tend to divide their inquiry into several foundational beliefs or interrelated topics. These central theological foci include

☐ God (theology proper)

☐ humankind and the created universe (anthropology)

□ Jesus and the salvation he brought (Christology)

□ the Holy Spirit and the Spirit's work in us and in the world (pneumatology)

□ the church as the fellowship of Christ's disciples (ecclesiology)

□ the consummation or completion of God's program for creation (eschatology)

Good theology begins by exploring these topics as they are informed by faith in Jesus, who is the revelation of God.

Why Theology?

A central goal of theology is to understand and describe what we believe as Christians, what we hold to be true given our faith in Jesus Christ. Since the first century the church has affirmed the importance of theology to its mission. And Christians have defined theology according to the role it plays in the church's task. We engage in theological reflection because theology assists *us* in being Christ's disciples, and we can understand theology in accordance with the assistance it is designed to give.

What is theology's role in the life of discipleship? What does good theology do? We can capsulize our answer in one sentence: Good theology assists Christians because it grounds their lives in biblically informed, Christian truth.

To understand this, consider a key aspect of the context of life today: This is a pluralistic world in which each person is continually bombarded with assertions as to what is ultimately true. A discordant chorus of voices arises, each claiming to inform people as to what they should believe and each inviting hearers to embrace the "truth" it proclaims.

Confused by the variegated claims to ultimacy that come their way, many people have embarked on a spiritual and intellectual odyssey. En route on this journey of discovery, they flit from one belief to another, depending on what happens to be the fad of the day. Perhaps yesterday it was transcendental meditation. Maybe today it's New Age spirituality. And who knows what tomorrow may bring? But whatever it is, be assured, these "pilgrims" will be part of it.

The ill-fated, short-lived television series *Amazing Grace,* which aired in 1995, embodies this mood. Although borrowing its name from the grand old evangelical hymn, the program features a female cleric, Hanna Miller, who is neither Protestant nor Catholic. As viewers would expect, Hanna's "call" to her nondescript ministry came in a nontraditional manner; it followed on the heels of a divorce, an addiction to prescription drugs and a near-death experience. Again as viewers would expect, the program downplays any specific religious ties Hanna may hold, replacing them with a focus on a generic spirituality.

Although a fictitious character—the product of some scriptwriter's psyche—Hanna fits the profile of the lead actress, Patty Duke. Listen to Duke's account of her own spiritual pilgrimage: "I was born into a Roman Catholic family. I have been a Christian Scientist. I have studied Buddhism. I studied to convert to Judaism. I think you can see a trend here. So it's not all that odd to me that I should wind up playing a minister on television. I'm as lost as anybody else. And I'm as found as anybody else."[2]

Amazing Grace reflects the ethos of today. To many people, the search for truth as embedded in the one true religion is passe. What is "in" is the quest for spirituality. And this quest, they claim, may lead through a variety of religious traditions, each of which offers *some* insight. Their advice? Just remember that no religion holds the final answer. Each religious expression is merely a way station along the path. So move with the times from one religious fad to the next!

The Christian's desire to avoid being swept along by the ever-changing currents that blow across the landscape should lead to theology. In the context of competing visions, Christian theology seeks to articulate Christian truth. Theology instructs Christians as to what belongs to the distinctively Christian teaching about God and the world. As they come to see what marks true belief (orthodoxy), they are able to detect and reject false teachings (heresy). By grounding us in *the truth*, theology contributes to our becoming mature, stable disciples of our Lord who are not "blown here and there by every wind of teaching" (Eph 4:14). Thus theology is vital to each Christian life.

Theology does, however, carry a certain "danger." It requires that we scrutinize our beliefs in the light of biblically informed Christian truth. In so doing, theology exercises a critical function (which we will explore in chapter five). As you test your beliefs, you may discover that certain things you assumed were true do not square with sound teaching. Your theological study leads you to jettison these long-held but incorrect convictions. This aspect of theology actually should strengthen your faith, not destroy it.

Solid Christian beliefs, in contrast, will stand the test of critical reflection. As they "pass muster," we will begin to hold them with even greater conviction. And other beliefs will be honed and clarified through theological study. As we come to understand such convictions with greater precision, our faith will be strengthened, for we will be able to affirm them with greater certainty.

As an example, consider the Christian teaching that God is triune—Father, Son and Holy Spirit. Perhaps to you this doctrine is little more than a mathematical puzzle: In some mysterious way God is one and three. You affirm this teaching, but not out of conviction borne by understanding; rather, because it is the "Christian" thing to do. In addition, perhaps your conception of the triune God focuses almost exclusively on God's oneness, as is evident, for example, in your prayers, which are routinely addressed to "God." Theological study should lead you to discover a greater richness in this traditional teaching. It should open your eyes to see that the one God is none other than Father, Son and Spirit—three distinct persons with distinct roles—united by mutual love.

When theology does its work, the doctrine of the Trinity—a teaching you once held tenuously—becomes a firm conviction. You now understand how the declaration "God is love" is inextricably bound to the teaching that God is Father, Son and Spirit. You see how the Christian conception is intellectually sublime in a way unparalleled in the understanding offered in any other religion. Never again will you be afraid to face the "evangelists" who come to your door with another gospel. Never again will you fear that they will shake your faith in what the church has taught about the triune God throughout the centuries. You now glory in and glorify God in God's own triunity.

This is how theology works. As Christians become more reflective and replace erroneous beliefs with correct convictions, and as they test and hone valid but imprecise and immature beliefs, they become even more steadfast in faith and more sure of what they believe. But the grounding work of good theology does not stop here.

Theology grounds Christian living. Because of the connection to the *what* and *why* of beliefs, many Christians view theology as a purely intellectual discipline. What is theology? For some, theology consists in dry debates about unimportant, unknowable or nonsensical points of doctrine. Theologians wonder about useless matters such as: Can God make a rock so heavy that he himself cannot lift it? Or, How many angels can stand on the head of a pin? They squabble with each other about potentially dangerous points of doctrine such as, Did God predestine the elect to salvation and the reprobate to condemnation before creating the world? To many Christians, such theological debate—and therefore theology and theologians in general—can only hinder their more important task, namely, sharing the gospel with the lost. Whether the damned "can't" or "won't" respond to the good news is in the end irrelevant, they declare. The sad fact is, the lost simply "don't."

This perception of theology is partially correct. Theologians do often appear to split hairs about seemingly inconsequential matters. While good theology does include academic debate, it never stops there. Good theologians discuss intellectual questions and concern themselves with academic debate because their chief concern is life. They want to know the truth not merely so that they might think properly, but so that they might live properly. They engage in theology not merely to amass knowledge, but also to gain wisdom. Good theology, therefore, brings the theoretical, academic, intellectual aspect of Christian faith into Christian living. In so doing, theology becomes immensely practical—perhaps the most practical endeavor one ever engages in!

In case you are wondering how such a heady discipline can actually be immensely practical, notice that there are several connections that give theology this practical, life-related dimension. First, theology is practical because it is inextricably linked to the most practical aspect of Christian life—its beginning point, that marvelous transaction we call "conversion."

To see this, let's ask what for many believers is the central question of our faith: What does it mean to be a Christian? The answer: A Christian is a person who is "converted." You and I claim to be Christians because we have encountered God in Christ in such a manner that our lives have been, are being, and will be radically changed. And this encounter places us in a new community, the people of God, the fellowship of Christ's disciples.

This encounter occurs through the hearing and believing of the gospel. But what exactly is the gospel? Many Christians would likely agree that at the heart of the good news is the biblical story of God's saving activity on behalf of sinful humankind. God has provided the way of salvation. And Christians all realize that to "call on the name of the Lord" (Rom 10:13), people must hear this salvation story.

Let's push our questioning a step further: Is the story itself sufficient to lead someone to Christ? Isn't something missing? Indeed! For people to believe the gospel, they must not only hear the story itself, they must also understand its meaning. Not only must people hear *that* Christ died and rose again—these brute facts of history do not yet bring us to the heart of the message—they must also be confronted with the *why* of his death and resurrection. They must understand that God acted in Christ for them.

The point is this: The biblical story always comes clothed in an interpretation that informs of the meaning of the events it narrates. This is how the gospel is found in the New Testament. The apostles and evangelists never merely retell the flat details of Jesus life, death and resurrection. They always tell the story in the context of its meaning: God was in Christ reconciling the world to himself, to cite Paul's interpretation (2 Cor 5:19). In the same way, the gospel declaration always comes clothed in theology. And this theology is not something additional to the gospel. It is an essential part of the good news.

For this reason, good theology sharpens our understanding of the gospel. It helps us clarify the meaning of the story of God at work in Christ. Theology does this so that we might declare the good news in a manner that people today can understand. And in so doing, theology serves the conversion process. It assists others in hearing the gospel so that they might meet the God who in Christ offers salvation to all.

This doesn't exhaust theology's link to conversion, however. Once people have committed their lives to Christ, they naturally desire to gain a deeper understanding of the God who has acted to save them, the God who has brought them into fellowship with himself and with other believers. Theology serves this quest. Theology wrestles with how best to conceive of and speak about the God who is the author and object of Christians' faith. In this pursuit, Christian believers raise questions such as: Who are we? What is it about the human situation that requires Christ's saving work? Who is Jesus, and how is he related to God? How does Jesus' death save us? What is the role of the Holy Spirit in the work of the triune God? What is faith all about? What does it mean to be a part of a redeemed people? Where is God taking us? Once we are believers we naturally want to know these things. Consequently, faith—conversion—readily leads to theology.

Theology's purpose does not end at conversion, however. It has a second practical goal in view: providing direction for Christian living. To see this, it is important to follow another line of reflection, which begins by asking, "What is the Christian life?" That's easy. All Christians would likely define the Christian life in terms of "discipleship." They might say that the Christian life is the attempt to live as Jesus' follower.

But what does it mean to "follow Jesus"? Although definitions might diverge at this point, Christian believers would likely agree that following Jesus is somehow connected to living "Christianly," living constantly aware that we are "little Christs," as the name *Christian* suggests. Believers might also agree that being a Christian involves loyalty to Jesus. We are a people who seek to "live out" our confession of allegiance to Christ. This answer, however, requires one further, crucial statement. Whatever else it may entail, loyalty to Christ includes living in accordance with a set of beliefs—a worldview—shaped by the biblical story of Jesus.

When we say "beliefs" or "worldview," we again step into the domain of theology, for theology explores the Christian belief system, or worldview. It sets forth the uniquely Christian understanding of all reality as this understanding arises from the story about Jesus of Nazareth. But theology doesn't merely articulate this understanding in the form of a series of statements or propositions that we claim are true. It doesn't stop with the great theological assertions—"God is love" or "Christ is fully God and fully human," for example—although such statements are an important aspect of theology.

Good theology moves beyond stating truths; it explores the significance of our beliefs or faith assertions for all of life. Theology asks questions such as: What are the implications of the doctrine of the Trinity for the way we pray? Or, What does the affirmation of Jesus' full humanity have to do with how I conduct myself on Monday morning?

By exploring these matters, theology provides Christians with needed direction as they seek to live as Christ's disciples. Of course, Christians also pursue theology so that they might gain a greater understanding—even a more systematic understanding—of their faith. But this is not their ultimate purpose. Good theology always makes a difference in how Christians live, and it motivates them as well. As they come to know more about God and his relationship to the world, disciples of Christ are drawn to love God more. As they come to love God more, they desire to serve him more. Good theology always moves from the head to the heart and finally to the hand.

To see how this works, consider again the teaching that God is triune. When exploring the doctrine of the Trinity, we discover that throughout eternity the Father loves the Son, and the Son reciprocates the love of the Father. But this is not mere intellectual theorizing. We learn as well that as the Son, Jesus reveals how people should respond to God. God is their loving Father who created them to give back this love to him. At this point the Holy Spirit steps in. When people are born again, the Spirit indwells them. And this indwelling Spirit draws believers into the glorious relationship the Father and the Son share, for the Spirit causes them to know God as their loving heavenly Father (Gal 4:6) just as Jesus did.

The implications of this realization are immense. The doctrine of the Trinity helps Christians understand how they are to come before God in prayer: They may pray to the Father in the name of the Son and by the prompting of the Spirit. Likewise the doctrine of the Trinity affords an entirely new perspective on who believers are and why they are here: They are children of the heavenly Father whose purpose is to live to the praise of their Maker and Redeemer. Knowing the dynamics of conversion in the light of the eternal relations of Father, Son and Spirit, causes believers' hearts to well up with a love that translates into willing service. Just think of the great privilege you have: The Spirit draws you into the glorious relationship the Son enjoys with the Father. Should you not love and serve a God who is so gracious?

"Who needs theology?" we ask. The answer is clear: All do. Theology seeks to clarify and articulate Christian doctrine, but its goal is wider. Christians engage in theological reflection so that their lives might be changed. Theological reflection ought to foster godly spirituality and obedient discipleship. Indeed, good theology will make believers stronger, better informed, and consequently, more effective disciples. Therefore, we must add to our earlier definition of theology: Christian theology is reflecting on and articulating the beliefs about God and the world that Christians share as followers of Jesus Christ *for the sake of Christian living.*

Theology pleases God. We engage in theology because theological reflection grounds our lives in biblically informed Christian truth. It fosters maturity so that we might be stable believers in the shifting sands of our day and fosters wisdom so that we might live as disciples.

So far our discussion has focused on Christian believers. We have defined theology by looking at what theological reflection does *for us.* As a result, our definition has been anthropocentric, *human-centered.* Anthropocentric theology, however, is ultimately insufficient. We dare never engage in theology merely for what it can do for us, as helpful and important as that may be. By its very nature, theology must always lift people's eyes above themselves—even above themselves as Spirit-indwelt Christians—and focus on the triune God. Theology must be theocentric, *God-centered.* So also our definition of theology must in the end move beyond ourselves as humans and believers and find its resting place in God. What, then, would a theocentric defini-tion of theology look like? We have already forged a link between theology and discipleship. We must now strengthen this link, for this is the clue to a theocentric theology.

Jesus himself invited his disciples to engage in theology. He re-minded his disciples of the ancient commandment to love God with their *minds* (Mt 22:37; Mk 12:30; Lk 10:27). And Paul reiterated the Lord's admonition. He spoke about the importance of taking "captive every thought to make it obedient to Christ" (2 Cor 10:5). These biblical statements make clear that the life of discipleship is all-encom-passing.

Most Christians would acknowledge that discipleship includes their wills, emotions, intuitions, attitudes and actions. As Christians we realize that we are to serve God in all these aspects of our being. Where we sometimes stumble, however, is with the mind. Yet discipleship includes the life of the mind as well (Mt 22:37). Christ wants to be Lord of our minds (2 Cor 10:5).

A first impulse might be to connect Christ's lordship over the mind with the so-called thought life. Jesus wants his people to put away all evil, lustful or self-absorbed thoughts (see, for example, Mt 5:27-30), but this only scratches the surface. Individual thoughts are merely the symptoms of a deeper reality. Lying beneath them are the core convictions—the belief structure, the worldview—that govern not only thoughts but also entire lives. Discipleship means allowing Christ to be Lord of these. It entails sharing the core convictions displayed in the life of Jesus the Lord. Hence Christians sing, "May the mind of Christ, my Savior, live in me from day to day. . . ."

Theological reflection is a crucial aspect of disciplining the mind. As people seek answers to the great questions about the Christian belief system, they engage in the task of bringing their convictions into conformity with God's own truth.

How does this process lead to a theocentric theology? One answer seems obvious: Godly convictions lead to godly living, and godly living glorifies God. Thus, the final goal of theological reflection is that God might be glorified through believers' lives, through how they live and what they do.

Yet the response runs deeper. Good theology results in God being glorified even in believers' minds themselves. Theological reflection leads to thinking rightly about God as well as about oneself and about the world as a creation under God. This pleases God. In fact, even the quest to know truth, when it is motivated by the desire to obey the Lord in every aspect of life, pleases God.

Therefore, as Christ's obedient disciples—as those who would honor God with their minds—Christians can joyfully offer their theologizing and their theological discoveries to God as acts of worship. Good theology is one vehicle whereby believers can love God with their minds.

Theology doesn't only enhance personal glorifying of God, however. It functions in the Christian community in the same manner, coming to expression in every aspect of community life. Most significantly, theology shapes corporate worship. It is embodied in the music sung and played, in the words spoken, in the symbolic acts employed, and even in the structure of worship. Good theology leads to good worship, and good worship glorifies God.

Again we ask, "Who needs theology?" In a direct way, you and I do. And we do together. But in a special way, God does. God doesn't actually *need* theology in the strict sense, because the triune God is complete within the eternal divine life. But God chooses to need theology. God has decided to inhabit his people's praises (Ps 22:3), which means that the eternal, triune God condescends to "inhabit" good theology, for through this seemingly insignificant human endeavor, God is praised and glorified.

Given all of this understanding, we can now offer a more complete definition of good theology: Christian theology is reflecting on and articulating the God-centered life and beliefs that Christians share as followers of Jesus Christ, and it is done in order that God may be glorified in all Christians are and do. *Soli Deo gloria.*

4

Defending Theology

I (Stan) had worked at the Northwest Church for three years as youth director during my seminary training. Now I was preparing to leave for graduate studies in Germany. One day a dear saint offered this admonition: "Don't let that theology professor destroy your faith!" My Christian friend was concerned that any further study of theology would undermine the firmness of my Christian convictions and deaden my zeal for serving the Lord.

Perhaps my friend's admonition expresses exactly what you are thinking: *Given the dangers formal study of theology may pose, who really needs theology?* If this is your concern, you are not alone. Even many Christian leaders and educators have expressed similar concerns about theology as a formal discipline.

When Bethany College in West Virginia began as a Christian educational institution in the nineteenth century, its revivalist founder wrote into its charter that it would never have a professorship of theology and that its main textbook would always be the Bible.[1]

Whether they have gone so far as to ban theology in the charter or not, numerous other Bible colleges and Christian institutions of higher learning have also shunned serious, reflective study of theology in their curricula.

Whence this antipathy to theology among Christians? We have already alluded to it in some detail and hinted strongly at some of its sources and supports: anti-intellectualism, folk theology, experiential-subjective religion, arid and sterile academic theology, lack of practical translation of theological ideas, and poor interactions between laypeople, pastors and professional theologians.

Theological studies undoubtedly can be an enemy of faith, but the antidote to bad theology is not no theology; it is good theology. Contrary to what some people suggest, there are no simple believers who remain untainted by theology, for all are theologians. Therefore, the question is not "Will we be theologians?" but "Will we be good theologians?"

Since we have already defended theology, another chapter devoted to that cause may seem unnecessary. However, we believe there is point and purpose to pausing here—after defining theology—to defend it once again in depth and detail.

Perhaps you are a bit confused about why theology is so controversial. The reason becomes clear once we step back and reflect on the situation for a moment. There are different ideas of theology and different levels of theology. So far we have made quite clear what we understand theology to be—at least in its basic contours. We have also made clear that we believe there is validity in at least three distinct levels of doing theology—lay, ministerial and professional.

If one combines the definition of theology developed in chapter three with the type of theology labeled "lay theology" (or even the one labeled "ministerial theology") in chapter two and leaves it at that, perhaps there would be little objection to theology. The controversy arises when laypeople and pastors encounter professional theologians practicing the theology described and defined in the previous chapters—with a few added dimensions. We are not changing the definition developed in chapter three; rather, we are now suggesting that the definition itself implies some activities to which many "ordinary" Christians and pastors object.

What are these additional activities that raise objections to an otherwise largely unobjectionable discipline? At the end of chapter three we delivered our definition of theology: *Christian theology is reflecting on and articulating the God-centered life and beliefs that we share as followers of Jesus Christ, and it is done that God might be glorified in all we are and do.* This definition seems innocuous enough. Who could really object to it? On the surface it seems that such reflection and articulation is inevitable and necessary. However, once we attempt to plumb the depths of the words "reflecting on" and "articulating," we begin to run into those elements of professional theology to which many Christians object.

All the ramifications of reflecting on and articulating the fundamental beliefs about God and the world that make theology controversial will have to await explication in chapter five, "Theology's Tasks and Traditions." There we will go deeper into the activity of theology. But before we do that, we need to defend what we will explain there to be theology's tasks. We will show in a preliminary way what is involved in professional theology and why it is important, necessary and valuable. We will do so by adding some points to our definition of theology, building on the previous chapter and anticipating the next one, and then explaining why common objections to this sense of theology miss their mark.

Why Theology Is Controversial

The seemingly simple, straightforward definition of theology at the end of the previous chapter and repeated above is not really so simple or straightforward. What, after all, is truly involved in "reflecting on" and "articulating" fundamental beliefs about God and the world? Implied in the definition is the idea that there are preexisting beliefs on which we can reflect and articulate anew. No one theologizes in a vacuum by starting from scratch. Theology, whether lay, ministerial or professional, always begins with some body of beliefs and focuses on them in a critical and constructive way, examining their validity and attempting to articulate them in an intelligible manner to contemporary culture. These critical and constructive tasks of theology will become the subject of most of the next chapter.

It is especially the job of professional theologians to examine critically and to articulate anew already accepted beliefs—and this is what gets them in trouble with many good Christian people. Let's look at an example—one already begun in the previous chapter.

Christians have always held to something like the doctrine of the Trinity. Even first-century Christians thought about God's relationship with the world in terms of the Father's *Logos,* or Word, and Spirit acting as intermediaries between God and humanity. This belief, however, remained very inchoate—unformed and inarticulate—for centuries. Numerous misleading analogies and teachings grew up around it among Christians in the Roman Empire. Gradually (to make a very long and complicated story short) theologians began to reflect critically on what Christians believed in the light of Christian sources (biblical writings and apostolic teachings), Christian experience (prayer and worship), and contemporary culture (Greek philosophy) and to criticize certain ways in which Christians were expressing this fundamental belief.

It would be an understatement to say that the task of criticizing popular ideas of the Godhead and constructing a proper Christian doctrine of God's triunity brought controversy to theology! In fact, the first Christian Roman emperor—Constantine—who was a lay Christian and not a theologian, instigated the search for a proper theological definition and then turned against Athanasius, the very theologian who championed it against heretics, for refusing to compromise the definition in a way that would have destroyed it.

Ever since that time in Christianity's infancy, theology has played a controversial role because of its tasks of critical reflection and constructive articulation of fundamental beliefs. In the example cited above regarding the Trinity, Athanasius was exiled by emperors five times for refusing to agree to add one tiny mark—the equivalent of the letter *i*—to the Greek word for Jesus' unity with God: *homoousios.* The opponents of the Nicene Creed, which had defined the unity of Jesus with God using that term, which means "of the same substance," wanted to alter it to *homoiousios*—"of similar substance"—meaning that Jesus is semidivine and not "truly God."

Athanasius's refusal has been criticized by some historians who have accused him of tearing the Roman Empire apart over one letter. To them, this controversy and theologian Athanasius's role in it are the epitome of theological hairsplitting! Most Christians down through the centuries, however, would say that everything about the Christian gospel depends on Jesus' unity with God—that is, with his "deity." They would therefore applaud Athanasius's firmness in refusing to change one tiny iota. Without his tenacity we would not have the doctrine of the Trinity with all its practical benefit for prayer and worship as explained in chapter three above.

As any student of church history knows, however, there are plenty of counterexamples to Athanasius—examples of instances in which theological firmness amounted to little more than stubborn hairsplitting. One notorious, but probably apocryphal, example comes from Constantinople in the fifteenth century. While the city's gates were being battered down by invading Muslim armies bent on destroying the last vestige of the old Christian Roman Empire, Eastern Orthodox theologians and leaders were allegedly sitting in the great Hagia Sophia cathedral debating how many angels can dance on the head of a pin.

The point we are trying to make is simply this: our definition of theology is sufficient but not exhaustive as an explanation of all that professional theology is and does. An old saying is that "the devil is in the details." To many of theology's detractors, its dangers appear only when professional theologians begin working out the details of critical and constructive examination of beliefs. Yet even those details of theology's critical and constructive tasks are necessary and valuable when kept within proper limits. Reflection on the conflicting beliefs held by Christians necessarily involves criticizing some of those beliefs. They cannot all be true. Many are contradictory, and many arise out of wishful thinking. Others are simply proven false or inadequate by further study of Scripture.

Articulation of Christian beliefs anew necessarily involves attempting to construct new formulations of the Christian faith and bringing each doctrine into some kind of coherent, systematic whole with all other Christian beliefs. The only alternative to this controversial process is to fall back into folk theology in which everyone believes whatever seems right in his or her own eyes and Christianity loses persuasive force and influence.

Having built on the basic definition of theology in chapter three, and anticipating its further elaboration in chapter five, we now move on to defend formal, professional theology and its value for the development of lay and ministerial theology.

Objections to Theology

Everyone who has been around Christian churches and institutions for very long is familiar with some of the pervasive objections to theology. These can be helpfully summed up in four major perennial objections: the Killjoy Objection, the Divisiveness Charge, the Speculation Accusation and the Stalemate Indictment.

Every theologian is familiar with versions of the *Killjoy Objection.* Among them are statements or questions such as: "Aren't God and his Word meant to be enjoyed? And doesn't theology just examine them to death and take all the life out of the Christian's relationship with God?" No doubt this is the objection the radio preacher had in mind when he declared, "Happy is the Christian who has never met a theologian!" Many Christians picture theologians, professional or lay, as hopeless killjoys bent on taking all the fun out of being Christian.

Linus van Pelt, the child theologian of the *Peanuts* comic strip, sometimes tends to reinforce this stereotype of the professional theologian. As he carefully puts the finishing touches on a snowman, Charlie Brown walks toward him asking, "Well, Linus, did you have a good Christmas?"

"What do you mean by 'good'?" Linus replies. "Do you mean did I get a lot of presents? Or do you mean did I give a lot of presents?"

As Charlie Brown stands perplexed, Linus waxes eloquent with arms thrown wide. "Are you referring to the weather or the Christmas dinner we had? Do you mean was my Christmas good in a spiritual sense?"

Finally, Charlie Brown heaves a sigh of exasperation as Linus continues: "Do you mean was my Christmas good in that I saw new meaning in old things? Or do you mean . . . ?"

Besides *Peanuts,* where does this deeply ingrained perception of dour, needlessly complicated theology come from? A possible source is a bias toward the subjective and emotional among many Christians. That is, the popular pietist and revivalist strands of modern Protestant Christianity have led many believers to conclude that the primary thing about being a Christian is having certain feelings. Whether or not they are connected to objective truth is secondary at best.

Such thinking is a distortion of true pietism and revivalism. Neither the great leaders of the pietist movement nor those of the great revivals of modern church history reveled in sheer subjective feeling divorced from truth. Numerous Christians have, however, gained the impression that being a Christian is primarily about having certain emotional experiences and feelings.

Theology's critical task can be greatly disillusioning to persons who attach strong emotional commitments to inadequate or false interpretations of biblical texts or who center their devotional lives on songs and choruses or around teachings of television evangelists that turn out under examination to be misleading if not downright heretical.

The theologian who brings these things to light is not often thanked for it!

The Killjoy Objection can betray a subtle but dangerous misunderstanding of Christianity that lowers it to the level of superstition. If the main benefit of Christianity is feeling good, and if anything that detracts from that joy or comfort is automatically suspected of being unspiritual, then how does Christianity differ from a cult or from drugs or psychotherapy? One major way in which Christianity surely differs from these is that it makes truth claims. It purports to be based on a narrative about reality—God's self-revelation and historical salvation of people. In that case, however, feelings should adjust to reality—not the other way around.

I (Roger) was having breakfast with a diverse group of men—some Christians and some not. The discussion turned to what the Bible teaches about life after death. One young man expressed strong belief in reincarnation. It turned out that his wife had died a few months before, and believing that she lived in another body now helped him cope with the loss. After he left, a number of the Christian men began to discuss belief in reincarnation. One of them said, "If that is what brings someone closer to God and their departed loved ones, then so be it—it's true for that person. No one has a right to say it isn't."

When I attempted to explain that reincarnation is incompatible with other Christian beliefs and with the entire teaching of the biblical narrative about Jesus Christ who died and was raised, this man and a few others objected. "You theologians! You're always trying to tell people how they should think. What really matters is how you feel in your heart, and if your heart tells you reincarnation is true, then who's to say otherwise?"

The result is that "Christianity" becomes compatible with any and every belief and thus becomes meaningless except as a folk religion based entirely on subjective emotions and personal states of mind. It is disconnected from truth and reduced to a matter of preference.

Another common version of the Killjoy Objection against professional theology is "Why examine everything? Why not just have simple faith? Aren't we supposed to be like little children and not question everything?" Indeed, this may be the kind of objection to formal theologizing most often heard by theology teachers! People who raise this objection often point to Jesus' acceptance of little children when he held them up as examples of those who would enter God's kingdom. They conveniently overlook that the apostle Paul commended the Christians of the city of Berea because they examined the new gospel of Christ in the light of the Hebrew Scriptures before accepting it as true (Acts 17:11). Both childlike faith and critical examination have a place in Christianity.

Too many people confuse "simple, childlike faith" with "simplistic and childish faith." Theology—even professional theology—does not deny the necessity of humble acceptance of God's message to humankind in Jesus Christ and the scriptural narrative about him. It does, however, push beyond blind and unquestioning acceptance of any and every interpretation of that message that happens to sound spiritual or comforting.

Emil Brunner, a great twentieth-century Swiss theologian, offered a marvelous illustration in answer to the Killjoy Objection in its various forms. He compared the gospel to fresh produce in a market. The fruits and vegetables are there to be enjoyed by the palate and to nourish people's bodies, not to be cut up and examined by instruments in a laboratory. Yet no one objects to the fact that some of the fruit is so examined in modern laboratories! It must be examined to assure that the produce is safe and wholesome. The health department sends inspectors around to the markets to take samples back to their laboratories to analyze them for poisons, nutritional value, freshness and so on. In the process of being broken down and examined, they are necessarily destroyed—but all for the sake of the consumers' health.

Likewise, theology may look as if it is destroying belief, but in reality it is examining and testing Christian beliefs and teachings to find out if they are consistent with good spiritual health. The litmus test is Jesus Christ and the biblical message that centers around him. Just as engaging in laboratory analysis of food is no substitute for eating, so theological examination of beliefs is no substitute for full-orbed Christian faith. The theologian—like the food expert—should be a connoisseur and not merely a critic. Just as the connoisseur should not complain against the food tester, arguing that produce is to be eaten and not analyzed, so the faithful Christian should not complain against the theologian, announcing that beliefs are to be accepted and never examined. Some beliefs, like some produce, are inimical to good health.

The second common objection to formal theology is the *Divisiveness Charge*. This one has even been formulated in a slogan: "Jesus unites; theology divides."

I (Roger) had just finished delivering a talk at a Christian coffeehouse about a popular new religious movement whose emissaries had arrived in town. The emissaries themselves showed up and sat in the front row. I had made it my business as associate pastor of the church sponsoring the coffeehouse to read as many of the group's founder's books as possible and to search out secondary sources about him as well. My research had convinced me without a doubt that this group's message was a "false gospel." Its advocates talked as much like Christians as possible, but their literature revealed that their founder believed in many occult ideas and practices, and reincarnation was central to their system of beliefs. Worst of all, they did not believe that Jesus Christ is uniquely God incarnate or that salvation comes by God's grace through faith.

After expounding and explaining the heresies of this new religious movement to the denizens of the coffeehouse, I went out and stood on a busy sidewalk and talked with various people who had attended the session. The cultists stood right next to me to monitor everything I said. They had earlier delivered a veiled threat of a lawsuit if I said anything wrong about their "church." Soon they engaged me in earnest debate. We heatedly, but civilly, discussed in front of others whether or not their movement should be considered authentically Christian.

Just at the moment when I was beginning to turn young, impressionable minds away from sympathy with this group, a pickup truck came screeching to a halt right in front of us. A man hopped out and joined our little circle. After just a few moments, he jumped into the fray and grabbed both me and one of the cultists by our arms. "Do you love Jesus?" he said right into my face. "Yes," I replied. "Do you love Jesus?" he said to the cultist. "Yes," the man predictably replied. "Then let's stop all this arguing and just love one another!" the man demanded.

Fortunately, that particular cult did not gain a strong foothold in that town, no thanks to the pious objector to theological discussion! Like so many who proclaim the slogan "Jesus unites; theology divides," he played right into their hands. Even Satan, we are told, masquerades as an angel of light (2 Cor 11:14). Sometimes theology can play a role in revealing the true nature of a disguised demon.

There is a kernel of truth in the objection that theology sometimes unnecessarily divides Christians. Every student of church history knows well the horror stories of churches and denominations splitting over minute details of doctrine. One sixteenth-century Anabaptist group in Europe is supposed to have split over the issue of wearing buttons or hooks on men's overcoats! (Even then there was some purpose to the debate. It was not merely about buttons and hooks but about how much Christians should look like the military, which had recently adopted the practice of wearing buttons. The Anabaptists were pacifists and rejected war.) Other renewal movements have split over instrumental versus vocal music in church, details of the expected second coming of Jesus Christ, and numerous other matters that most Christians would consider fairly unimportant.

The truth in the objection does not make the objection completely valid, however. While it is true that "Jesus unites," it is also true that "Jesus divides." Jesus himself said, "Do not suppose that I have come to bring peace to the earth. I did not come to bring peace, but a sword"

(Mt 10:34). Not all of Jesus' words were sweetness and light. We should be careful not to pit Jesus against truth.

Also, while it is true that sometimes theology divides, it is also true that sometimes theology unites! Many divided Christian denominations have held dialogues during which they have discovered more in common than they had thought (or feared!). Out of many such dialogues have come newly united or reunited Christian denominations. This too is a work of theology.

The main answer to the Divisiveness Charge against theology is that the primary purpose of theology is neither to divide nor to unite, but to discover and protect truth. Martin Luther once declared, "Peace if possible, but truth at any cost!" and that must be theology's motto.

A third complaint against theology is the *Speculation Accusation.* Unfortunately, many Christians have the impression that the main occupation of theologians is useless speculation. This accusation has two prongs. On the one side it charges that theology delves too deeply into mysteries that are simply beyond human understanding. On the other side it charges that in this preoccupation with the unknowable, theology loses touch with practical, everyday reality.

Once again *Peanuts* provides an illustration. This time it is Charlie Brown who embodies the stereotype.

"I have a theological question," Linus says to Charlie Brown. As they stand looking over a brick wall with arms folded and clouds floating behind their heads, Linus continues earnestly, "When you die and go to heaven, are you graded on a percentage or a curve?"

Charlie Brown answers, "On a curve, naturally."

Linus responds curiously, "How can you be so sure?"

To this, Charlie Brown, the speculative theologian, replies, "I'm always sure about things that are a matter of opinion."

Some theologians undoubtedly have attempted to reach beyond the grasp of human knowledge in understanding God's ways. In fact, I (Roger) was almost discouraged from becoming a theologian by this fault of some who practice my profession. While in college I was deeply enamored with courses in Bible and theology, but I felt that they only dabbled on the surface of deep questions whereas I wanted to go beneath that surface on my own. I went to a local Christian bookstore, asked for a volume of "serious theology" and was sold a fat tome on future things—events of Christ's second coming—written by a seminary professor who was a well-known expert on the end times, or eschatology. I took that book back to my dormitory room and began reading it. By the third chapter I was lost. I finally decided that I just wasn't sufficiently intellectually gifted to be a theologian. I simply could not figure out how the author got from point A (presupposed ideas) to point B (conclusion) and beyond. His conclusions about the events of the end times seemed to me to come out of nowhere! I was dismayed by my lack of understanding.

Later, after I had become a theologian in my own right, I returned to that book that so nearly diverted me from this vocation. Now I recognize the author as a theologian who simply thinks he knows more than human minds can know, given the meager information about the details of eschatology in the biblical message. No doubt twentieth-century American theologian Reinhold Niebuhr was right when he said that we should not want to know too much about the furniture of heaven or the temperature of hell! Too many theologians have claimed to know more than can be known about these and many other things.

However, that is not the entire story. As theologians and teachers of Christian theology, we have encountered many students and church people who are reluctant to follow the clues of divine revelation where they genuinely can lead them. While no one can think God's thoughts after him, God has left a sufficient witness in history, nature, Scripture and the community of God's people so that devout reason working with these sources and tools can discover genuine, if always incomplete, knowledge about God. For the sake of the church and its worship and witness, this knowledge needs to be unified into a body of justified Christian beliefs. Some of those beliefs will inevitably seem unjustified—speculative—to Christian people who have not bothered to follow the line of thinking that has led from divine revelation through reasonable interpretation to explanation. Christians who do take the time and trouble to explore the processes and products of theological reflection find their Christian faith strengthened with mental conviction.

The final major objection to formal theology is the *Stalemate Indictment*. A stalemate arises when a process becomes stuck and no further progress is possible. Many Christians believe that in spite of much activity theology makes no real progress.

This complaint is somewhat more sophisticated than the first three. One does not often hear it except from those who have attempted study of theology at some level and given up out of frustration or disillusionment. Specifically, this complaint argues that after the formative stages of Christian theology in the first few centuries, the discipline of theology became mainly critical and has failed to achieve progress through constructive solutions to problems. To this way of thinking, theologians are very adept at criticizing Christian beliefs but hardly ever go beyond that to providing helpful new solutions to old theological dilemmas in such a way that these solutions become the consensus within the churches.

When reading Charles Schulz's *Peanuts* comics, one has to wonder if he feels this way about theology. The Stalemate Indictment is implicit in Sally's oral essay: "My topic today is the purpose of theology." She continues as she authoritatively holds up one finger: "When discussing theology we must always keep our purpose in mind." With eyes piously shut she explains to the class, "Our purpose as students is understandably selfish." Then she adds, "There is nothing better than being in a class where no one knows the answer."

The Stalemate Indictment is the most difficult of the four challenges for theologians to answer because it so much depends on what one would count as "progress." The objector often expects nothing less than Christian consensus. There are over one billion Christians in the world separated into at least three major divisions (as will be discussed in the next chapter), which in turn are separated into hundreds of denominations and religious orders. It is difficult to imagine how consensus could be achieved among Christians except in such a slow and gradual manner as to be barely perceptible.

If what is expected, then, is swift, observable, sweeping changes in Christian beliefs that almost overnight solve dilemmas that have baffled and perplexed Christians for centuries, the standard is too high. There are, however, instances in which theological reflection brings forth new ways of looking at old problems that gradually lead to partial solutions to what seemed like doctrinal stalemates. Examples could be cited from the early church and the Reformation. Actually, many who raise the Stalemate Indictment would readily admit that in these formative periods theology did achieve some real progress—but not since then, they argue. Offering examples from more recent times poses a problem, since the church of Christ has been more divided in the last four to five hundred years (since the Reformation) than before. Achieving consensus for solutions to old problems is nearly impossible.

One problem that bedeviled Christian thinkers from the early church through the nineteenth century had to do with God's relationship to the sufferings of his creatures—especially human beings created in God's own image. Most Christians assumed that it would be improper to attribute suffering to God, yet how could God not suffer with creatures if God is a loving heavenly Father? Almost all branches of Christianity, however, taught that God is incapable of suffering because suffering is something creaturely, not divine. This placed a question mark over God's compassion. The same Christians who denied God's ability to suffer affirmed God's compassion toward human beings. Yet compassion means "suffering with." A true dilemma!

The great medieval theologian Anselm of Canterbury tried to break through this dilemma by arguing that God's compassion is not something that God feels, for this would imply that God suffers, which would detract from God's absolute perfection. Instead compassion is something that we humans feel when we contemplate God's perfection in our suffering.

Although the great Reformer Martin Luther strongly hinted at God's suffering in the cross of Jesus Christ, most Protestant theologians went along with the centuries-old assumption that God-in-himself cannot suffer. But something changed in the middle of the twentieth century. In fact, some have come to speak of the idea of the suffering of God as a "new orthodoxy" that almost no one dares to challenge or question. A few Christian leaders and theologians may question whether this is an example of "progress" in theology, but there can hardly be doubt that it represents a major breakthrough—a paradigm shift—in reflection about God and God's relationship with the world.

How did this development occur? Who brought it about? While many factors contributed to it, the major cause was theological reflection on Christian sources in the light of contemporary experiences. After the Holocaust and Hiroshima, Christian thinkers around the world began to explore the meaning of God's relationship to suffering human beings. These theologians discovered that the God of Jesus Christ is not the impassive God of much traditional theology, but the God who suffers the pain of people.

One of the first books to explain this new idea of God came from the pen of a Japanese Christian in the aftermath of World War II. Kazoh Kitamori wrote *Theology of the Pain of God*[2] to suggest that the best *Christian* way to conceive of God in the light of both the New Testament and modern experiences is as a suffering God.

This idea caught on rapidly and was explored further and promoted widely by German theologian Jürgen Moltmann, who connected God's suffering closely to the cross of Christ as well as to twentieth-century horrors. Others picked up on the idea, and it soon became an accepted part of Christian thinking about God across a broad spectrum of churches and types of theologies. It still has and always will have its detractors, but universal agreement is never a necessary condition for true progress.

Thus we have one example of progress in theology—so long as one does not define progress as universal agreement on a new solution to an old problem. That is hard to imagine without a universal "magisterium," a theological supreme court. Only the Roman Catholic Church has a magisterium, and it is not recognized by Eastern Orthodox, Protestant or sectarian Christian groups. The point of the example is simply this: whereas most Christians thought the idea of God's suffering was almost blasphemous for over one thousand years, in a matter of a few decades a small handful of theologians convinced most Christians that God's suffering is gospel truth.

Some Christians will not recognize this change as progress, and many others will look for change or progress in other theological matters. For example, many of theology's detractors will not be satisfied until there is a major, convincing breakthrough in the old divine sovereignty-human freedom dilemma. For centuries Christians have wondered and theologians have debated how God can be sovereign (all-determining Lord of history) and humans be free and responsible. Although many solutions have been proposed, none has gained universal acceptance. But focusing on this dilemma as proof that theology never achieves real progress is like focusing on the fact that medical science has no cure for the common cold as proof that it never experiences breakthroughs. Concern over lack of progress in one area should not blind people to real achievements in other areas.

As we acknowledged earlier, the Stalemate Indictment will always remain the most difficult complaint for theologians to answer. The reasons for that are obvious to theologians, but perhaps not so obvious to others. Given that we humans "see through a glass darkly" until we see Christ face to face, and that there is no universal power of persuasion or enforcement within the Christian community, and that people will always tend to focus on the yet-unresolved problems rather than the already-solved ones, it is not surprising that this objection remains strong among theology's detractors. We can only hope that as you continue to explore theology you will come to realize that real progress is possible. As a result you will learn to be patient with its snail's pace.

In this chapter we have attempted to answer some of the complaints Christians lodge against formal theology. We have gone beyond the simple and straightforward definition of theology offered in chapter three without abandoning it. And we have made clear that implied in this definition are some practices that many well-meaning Christians find objectionable. We have defended these practices *before* exploring them in depth and detail—the task of our next chapter.

But we don't wish to leave the impression that we would defend every theologian or way in which theology past or present goes about its tasks. That would be entirely wrong. All we want to defend here—and throughout the book—is *the discipline and practice of theology itself.* We do object to specific theologians and their ways of doing theology. (See, for example, our book *20th-Century Theology: God and the World in a Transitional Age* [Downers Grove, Ill.: InterVarsity Press, 1993], in which we strongly criticize certain individual theologians and trends in theology in the "modern" age.) But we object just as strongly to any suggestion that theology itself—when rightly practiced—is spiritually deadening, unnecessarily divisive, merely speculative or ineffective.

5

Theology's
Tasks & Traditions

*O*ne day during my first year of teaching, I (Roger) had just returned to my office after lecturing in the course "Christian Theology" when a student knocked at my door and asked to speak with me privately. She was struggling with theology and felt the need to express her frustrations. I understood and sympathized with her as she poured out those negative emotions.

Her main purpose in coming, however, was to criticize my style of teaching theology, and her specific comment took me aback—though I have since become accustomed to hearing it. "Why don't you just tell us what the truth is about every subject we study?" she asked. "It confuses us when you present several options and leave it up to us to decide what to believe. Even when you tell us your own opinion and give reasons for it, you leave it up to us too much, as if there could be several possible ways of interpreting that belief. You need to nail down the truth more clearly and firmly. That's why we're studying theology, isn't it? To learn the truth?"

I had just turned back to the tasks on my desk after the first student had left when a second student from the same class hesitantly knocked on my door. After being seated he explained his complaint about the course and my teaching style: "I feel that you concentrate too much on indoctrinating us. You know so much and have so many firmly held views that it doesn't leave much room for forming our own opinions. I wish you would just tell us what the options are and leave it up to us to come up with our own theological interpretations. After all, theology is just a bunch of individual opinions about God, isn't it?"

Needless to say, I was challenged by these contrasting criticisms. How could I teach a group of students with such diverse understandings of theology and expectations about how it should be taught?

In this chapter we will explore theology's tasks with the hope of alleviating some of the false expectations of and wrong impressions about theology. The first half of the chapter will be devoted to explicating theology's two major tasks—the critical and constructive tasks—and some specific activities involved in each one. The second half of the chapter will explain some of the major historical traditions of theology. The tasks are carried out in different ways by these different traditions.

In chapter three we defined Christian theology: *Christian theology is reflecting on and articulating the God-centered life and beliefs that Christians share as followers of Jesus Christ, and it is done that God might be glorified in all Christians are and do.* In chapter four we lightly touched on some of the implications of this definition for theology's activity and defended it against some common misconceptions and objections. Now we will unpack these activities or tasks more fully to make clearer exactly what theology *is* through explaining what it *does*. *Reflection* and *articulation* are rather vague and ambiguous terms. What do they imply for theology's specific tasks?

The two major tasks of theology are *the critical task* and *the constructive task*. The critical task includes two activities as does the constructive task. We will take each major task in turn and, after defining it, explain it through its activities.

Theology's Critical Task

Theology's critical task is to examine beliefs and teachings about God, ourselves and the world in light of Christian sources, especially the primary norm of the biblical message. This critical task occurred first in chronological order. That is, Christian theology—after the apostles' own teachings—began as defense of the gospel against false teachings within the Christian churches. It has rightly been said that "heresy is the mother of orthodoxy" and that "theologians owe more to the heretic than they often acknowledge." In other words, without heresy (false teaching) there would be no theology or orthodoxy (right teaching).

Even in the New Testament we see evidence that the apostles wrote primarily to correct wrong ideas and practices that arose in the early Christian churches. You need only read John's first epistle to see clearly that this is so. John, Jesus' youngest disciple and the one who lived longest, condemns false teachers, especially those who say that Christ did not "come in the flesh." Here is a strong hint of one early heresy that flared up dramatically in the second and third centuries among Christians. It became known as *docetism,* the belief that Christ only *appeared* to be human.

Theology's critical task, then, includes examining Christian teachings and beliefs for consistency with authentic Christian sources of truth. (We will discuss these sources in detail in chapter six.) This is its first activity. As we said earlier, Christians have always held beliefs about God, sin, salvation and so on. If you could have been among the two thousand or so Christians at the birth of the church on the day of Pentecost (Acts 2) and interviewed a number of them about beliefs, you would have found that all held certain ideas about important subjects related to God, Jesus Christ, salvation and so forth.

Theology does not invent beliefs; it finds beliefs already among

Christians and critically examines them. As we explained in chapter four, this is controversial to many people. "Why not just leave those beliefs alone?" they ask. Some answers have already been given, but one more is obvious: Even the apostles who wrote the New Testament did not do that! They heard of false beliefs among Christians and wrote letters to correct them.

Later Christian leaders did the same thing. Around A.D. 95—sixty years after Jesus' death—Clement, the bishop, or chief pastor, of the Christians at Rome, wrote a letter to the Christians at Corinth to correct their beliefs and behavior. Soon more and more Christian leaders, usually chief pastors of Christians in Greek and Roman cities, wrote letters and tracts against various false teachings in the infant churches.

One such group of heresies that had spread like wildfire and attacked the very core beliefs held dear by the apostles and their appointed successors was Gnosticism. It developed early and has stayed around in various forms. The Gnostics were self-proclaimed Christians in the Roman Empire who taught, among other things, that matter is evil, so it could not have been created by God. They also taught that Jesus Christ was neither God nor human but a divine messenger sent down from God to appear in a human body temporarily. He did not die on a cross, and his main purpose for coming was to teach a few especially worthy people the true way to salvation through self-knowledge. These Gnostics often set up semisecret orders of elite Christians, claimed to possess their own "secret sayings of Jesus" and "higher knowledge," and sometimes practiced secret rituals and ceremonies as alternatives to those practiced by ordinary Christians.

How could the church's leaders—some of whom may have been appointed by the apostles themselves—ignore this situation? In responding to it they "invented" theology! Many scholars of church history would argue that the first real Christian theologian was Irenaeus of Lyons, bishop of Christians in southern France at the end of the second century. Irenaeus spent years studying all the Gnostic sects and teachers and wrote five books responding to them, known as *Against Heresies*. He went into great detail exposing the fallacies of Gnostic teachings, and in the process he constructed some intriguing interpretations of apostolic teachings. So thorough and convincing was Irenaeus's writing that from then on the Gnostics struggled to maintain credibility; and some of Irenaeus's doctrinal interpretations, though not clearly spelled out in Scripture, were widely accepted as orthodox.

Ever since Clement and Irenaeus, toward the end of the first and second centuries respectively, the church has found it necessary to train people to inspect Christian teachings and ideas and decide whether they are sound or not. These are theologians. For the first several hundred years of the church's history, almost all theologians were also church leaders—priests or monks. There were a few exceptions, such as Tertullian, a lawyer of North Africa about the same time as Irenaeus, who wrote volumes exposing various heresies and recommending his own interpretations of sound Christian beliefs.

During the high Middle Ages the new universities gave rise to professional theologians who were teachers and not necessarily priests or monks. During the Modern Age (1650-1950) it has become more and more common for theologians to be ordinary lay Christians with training in biblical and theological studies. Some are ordained by a denomination without ever serving as pastor of a church. A few theologians have no obvious church ties. (This is true primarily of "academic theologians.")

Throughout two thousand years of church history, then, theologians have been actively engaged in studying the beliefs and teachings that parade as "Christian" to discover whether they really are Christian. It is no easy task, and sometimes a decision cannot be reached right away. Often debate goes on for a very long time.

During the nineteenth and twentieth centuries numerous people have acted as religious entrepreneurs founding their own religious sects—often called "cults"—on the basis of new "revelations" or new interpretations of the Bible. The same centuries have seen the rise of numerous new schools of thought among Christians and a proliferation of types of theologies that accommodate in some way to cultural beliefs. The theologians' task has been to examine, analyze, evaluate and recommend to the churches what beliefs to accept and which to reject. We will explore the criteria by which theologians judge beliefs in chapter six. As we said earlier, the litmus test is conformity to Jesus Christ and the biblical witness to and about him.

The second activity involved in theology's first task—the critical task—is to divide valid Christian beliefs into categories based on levels of importance. In other words, once a belief is determined to be valid—that is, consistent with authoritative Christian norms—the next question is "How important is it?" Is this a belief all Christians *must* hold in order to be authentically Christian? Or is this belief one on which Christians may legitimately disagree?

Over the centuries theologians have developed three main categories of Christian beliefs: *dogma, doctrine* and *opinion.* A belief is considered a dogma if it seems essential to the gospel. In other words, if its denial would seem to entail *apostasy*—rejection of the gospel of Jesus Christ—then it is a dogma. A doctrine, as the term is used here, is a belief that is considered important without being essential. That is, a particular Christian church or denomination may consider the belief a test of fellowship without claiming that its denial amounts to apostasy. The denial of a doctrine may be considered heresy but not necessarily outright apostasy. A belief is relegated to the status of opinion when it considered interesting but relatively unimportant to the faith of the church. One is allowed to believe whatever one wishes about the matter so long as it does not conflict with a dogma or doctrine. Denial of an opinion is simply a difference of interpretation.

Different Christian groups populate these categories with different beliefs, and that is one major reason for the existence of different denominations. One Christian denomination may consider belief in the virgin birth of Jesus Christ a dogma and treat anyone who denies it as a non-Christian, whereas another denomination may consider that belief a doctrine and simply require it for membership without claiming that it is absolutely necessary to being a Christian. A few denominations may even relegate it to the status of mere opinion. The point is that there is no universal categorization. The proper categorization is a constant matter of debate within and between Christian denominations, although there really is more agreement on this than many people suspect.

Now let us explore these categories one at a time. The *dogma* category was the earliest to evolve. In the early stages of theological reflection the critical task resulted in several key beliefs being accepted as absolutely essential to authentic Christian faith. The first place and time this officially happened was at the first universal council of the church known as Nicea I in A.D. 325. The first Christian emperor, Constantine, called all the bishops of Christian cities in the Roman Empire to meet in his home city of Nicea (next to his new capital city, Constantinople, which was still under construction) to discuss the argument over Jesus' divinity.

At Nicea the bishops wrote the first version of the Nicene Creed, which would later be revised into its full form at the second universal council, Constantinople I, in A.D. 381. The Nicene Creed stated that to be a Christian—especially a Christian leader—one absolutely must confess Jesus Christ as equal with God the Father as to eternal divine being and power (*homoousios,* "of the same substance"). Ever since then, Eastern Orthodox, Roman Catholic, and major Protestant churches have agreed that denial of the equality of Jesus with God the Father is tantamount to apostasy.

Later, other beliefs would be elevated to the status of dogma by major Christian councils of "undivided Christendom"—among them salvation by grace alone. But when the World Council of Churches (WCC) was founded as the major worldwide ecumenical umbrella organization for Christian cooperation in the twentieth century, it found universal agreement on only one dogma and stated it as its one and only test for admitting a church body—"Jesus Christ is God and Savior." Some churches and denominations refused to join the WCC partly because of this near emptying of the dogma category.

The second category, doctrine, contains beliefs that a particular tradition or denomination considers important enough to require as a criterion for membership. While denial of these beliefs does not necessarily strike at the heart of the gospel, it is judged to be implicit denial of the scriptural message and thus grounds for exclusion from fellowship. Common examples of items often listed as doctrine but not dogma are beliefs about predestination and free will, the sacraments or ordinances (baptism and the Lord's Supper), views on scriptural authority (inspiration, inerrancy), interpretations of church order (ecclesiology), and the events of the end times (eschatology). One rarely but occasionally finds these beliefs treated as dogmas.

I (Stan) was confronted with this distinction between dogma and doctrine during my seminary training. One day I was working feverishly on an assignment for theology class—namely, delineating a Christian understanding of the Trinity. The ringing of the doorbell interrupted my work. A Jehovah's Witness missionary was making his rounds in the neighborhood. I invited him in, and for close to two hours we discussed central matters such as Christ's deity, salvation by grace through faith, and, of course, God's triunity. The visit came to an abrupt end when I suggested that we pray together. My visitor quickly left after asserting that we would not be addressing the same God. The two of us were separated by fundamental differences—differences on the level of dogma.

The next year I was set to graduate. The statement of faith I submitted to the faculty as one of the graduation requirements received a concerned response. Was I intending to enter the pastoral ministry in the denomination of the seminary? If so, my eschatology would pose an insurmountable roadblock. My Christian identity was not at issue, but because I had moved away from the staunch premillennialism that was a doctrinal hallmark of the denomination, I would not be welcome in its pastorate. In the eyes of the concerned seminary faculty member our differences lay in doctrine, not dogma.

Finally, the third category, opinion, contains beliefs a particular denomination judges to be matters of private interpretation. Commonly left to this category are beliefs about details of eschatology (e.g., the pretribulational rapture), angels and demons, charismatic gifts and phenomena such as speaking in tongues (unless it is a Pentecostal denomination, in which case this becomes a matter of doctrine), and similar *adiaphora,* or things indifferent to the gospel.

One of the major activities of theologians, then, is to discover the proper location in this schema for each valid Christian belief. (Of course, if a belief is criticized as invalid or false, it is left out of the schema entirely.) This activity has provided plenty of grist for the theological mill, and some would like to stop the mill entirely. The only way to do that, however, is to relegate everything to opinion or dogma.

To avoid this hard task of properly ordering beliefs as to their relative importance to the Christian gospel, some churches and denominations have simply left everything to opinion. An example of a denomination that has explicitly embraced this "more tolerant" approach is the Unitarian-Universalist Fellowship of churches. It is dogmaless and doctrineless. The result is that people who strongly affirm that belief in the Trinity is necessary to authentic Christianity may find themselves out of that church. In a paradoxical way, churches that abolish all categories but opinion end up reinventing the categories by insisting that they stay empty as a test of fellowship. Emptying the categories actually becomes a new doctrine, which puts at least one belief back in the doctrine category, namely, the belief that there are no dogmas.

Other denominations have attempted to empty the opinion and doctrine categories so that every valid Christian belief is judged to be dogma. This alleviates the often painful and difficult process of properly locating beliefs but ends up in a cultish exclusivism in which anyone who does not agree with the denomination's particular stance regarding church government, for example, is considered apostate.

One fairly simple (and simplistic) way of beginning to grasp a major difference between liberal and conservative denominations is to recognize two tendencies in handling the indexing of beliefs. In general, more liberal theologians and denominations tend to empty the dogma and doctrine categories and leave more and more to the private judgment of individuals. Almost everything gets shoved into the opinion category. The Unitarian-Universalist denomination is the most liberal, but some so-called mainline denominations do much the same without announcing it or by calling it pluralism. Ultraconservative or fundamentalist theologians and denominations follow the opposite tendency. They empty the opinion and doctrine categories of most beliefs others would place there and fill up the dogma category.

Theology's Constructive Task
The second major task of theology, the constructive task, is to set forth the unity and coherence of the biblical teaching about God, ourselves and the world in the context in which God calls us to be disciples. This goes well beyond critically examining and categorizing Christian beliefs to attempting to construct and unify Christian doctrines and relate them faithfully and relevantly to contemporary culture.

Once again we will use the doctrine (dogma) of the Trinity to illustrate theology—this time theology's constructive task. As anyone who has spent time talking to a Jehovah's Witness knows, the word *Trinity* is not found in the Bible. In fact, the concept of God's three-in-oneness is nowhere explicitly formulated in Scripture. How, then, did it come to be a central tenet of Christianity?

The doctrine of the Trinity is a theological construct developed in early Christianity for two reasons directly related to and illustrative of theology's tasks. First, it was developed to guard the gospel of God in the flesh in Jesus Christ against subtle denials of Jesus' full and true deity (critical task). Second, it was developed further to explain to both Christians and non-Christians the sum of all that the biblical witness says about God. It is a defensive doctrine and a constructive doctrine.

As soon as anyone begins summarizing what Scripture teaches or implies about any subject, he or she is practicing theology's constructive task. Indeed, this enterprise is inevitable. It is impossible to imagine how any serious student of Scripture could avoid unifying the diverse expressions of the sixty-six books of the Bible on a given subject into some coherent whole. The doctrine of the Trinity, like many theological concepts, is simply a unifying model of God that attempts to pull together the biblical narrative's witness to the God revealed in Israel's history and in Jesus Christ into a coherent concept.

An example from arithmetic is helpful here.[1] On the surface, or to the uninitiated, the following numbers would seem to have little in common: $1/2$, $1/3$, $1/10$, $1/15$. Adding them up to get a whole number seems impossible. The same is true of the variety of biblical allusions to God. Sometimes God is described one way, sometimes another way. How it all adds up to the same God seems on the surface beyond all comprehension. However, the person trained in mathematics knows that adding the above fractions is simple: find the common denominator and translate them into $15/30$, $10/30$, $3/30$, and $2/30$. Their sum becomes $30/30$, or 1. With a little training a person can discern the unity of the biblical portrayals of and teachings about the biblical narrative's main character who otherwise seems elusive—God.

The doctrine of the Trinity is like the number 1 in the illustration— it is implicit in the raw materials but must be drawn out through a unification process. In a sense, then, the biblical witness does teach the Trinity, but only indirectly. The concept of Trinity is a product of synthesizing reflection on the diverse biblical portrayals of God. The Bible portrays God as one, but also as inwardly differentiated. The Bible portrays God as Father, Son and Holy Spirit, but also as perfectly unified. When all these aspects of the biblical picture of God are brought together—their common denominator recognized and made explicit—the result is the doctrine of the Trinity.

All the products of theology's constructive task, like the doctrine of the Trinity, may best be described as *models* of God and of God's relationship with the world. That is, they are not direct and literal *pictures* of God. So they are not scale or replica models, but analogue or disclosure models that have a structural similarity to the divine reality. A model of a molecule helps explain a theological model, the product of theology's constructive task. Chemists learn about compound molecules by making models out of colorful round pieces that snap together. No one should imagine that these models are simply larger-than-life replicas of molecules; they are analogues with structural similarities to molecules.

The products of theology's constructive task are such models. God and God's relationship with us cannot be literally pictured as "just exactly like" something else. God is transcendent, unique, not exactly like anything in creation. But because we must have ways of describing God and his relationship with us, we construct models that have some structural affinity to God and the God-world relationship. These are the doctrinal concepts theology constructs by unifying the otherwise diverse biblical expressions and portrayals of things divine.

The second activity of theology's constructive task is relating biblical models to contemporary culture. Theology's task is not complete when it has evaluated Christian beliefs, found them valid, and constructed unified models of biblical teachings. An all-important step remaining in theology's task is to package the models in intelligible ways so that contemporary people—Christian and non-Christian— can understand them.

While exploring the gift shop of an apple orchard, I (Roger) came upon a colorful booklet comparing God's triunity to an apple. As I flipped through the pages I recognized an attempt by some Christian author to convey something of the meaning of God's triune being to apple lovers. This author showed very visually and with few words

how an apple is one piece of fruit consisting of three distinct por-
tions—skin or peel, meat, and core. As a theologian I was not entirely
impressed; my critical task kicked in, and I began to evaluate this
comparison. Needless to say, it failed the test. Nevertheless, it was a
commendable effort on someone's part to make a theological model
relevant to certain people—in this case children—in a specific context.

On a more sophisticated level, many theologians have attempted to
explain the Trinity to contemporary people using images drawn from
psychological and social life. Recently, the "communitarian movement," a loose coalition of secular and religious people interested in
modifying American society's radical individualism and reasserting
individuals' obligations to communities, has provided some points of
contact for conveying the relevance of God's triune community to
people interested in overcoming individualism.

The task of contextualizing theology will be explored more fully in
chapter seven. For now we will simply say that this is one of theology's
most misunderstood and neglected activities, but without it theology
is in danger of falling into irrelevance and neglect.

Theology's tasks, then, are twofold or fourfold, depending on how
one looks at the rubric we have expounded here:

A. Theology's Critical Task
    1. Examining and Evaluating Christian Beliefs
    2. Categorizing Valid Christian Beliefs as Dogma, Doctrine or
       Opinion
B. Theology's Constructive Task
    1. Constructing Unified Models of Diverse Biblical Teachings
    2. Relating Those Models Relevantly to Contemporary Culture

Theology's Traditions

A part of understanding what theology is must be understanding the
various traditions within which it is practiced. Unfortunately, perhaps,
since at least the time of the schism between the Eastern Orthodox
family of churches and the Roman Catholic Church, theological re-

flection has been carried out in somewhat different ways depending on these communities' forms of life. Here we will provide brief sketches of four major historical theological traditions of Christianity and close with some cursory remarks about contemporary theology.

Some scholars of church history speak of the period before A.D. 1054 as "the time of the undivided church." While the first millennium of church history certainly saw various small schisms, visible, structural unity existed among all the bishops of the great Christian cities of the Roman Empire. (For the sake of brevity we must leave aside discussion of Christian communities in Asia and Africa of which very little is known from that time period.) Except for occasional disputes between them, which sometimes led to brief periods of excommunication of one bishop by another, the churches under Rome and Constantinople existed in fellowship.

Growing discontent and debate over the power and authority of the bishop of Rome and over exact definitions of the Trinity eventually led to a formal and final split between these two great Christian cities and their families of churches in A.D. 1054. No longer was there a "Great Church" undivided. Since then Western scholars have referred to these as the Eastern Orthodox and Roman Catholic traditions and churches. While they share much in common, they have marked differences that lead to different styles of theology.

The Eastern Orthodox churches believe that the first seven ecumenical councils of the undivided church (Nicea I in A.D. 325 through Nicea II in A.D. 787) constitute a definitive body of interpretations of Christian doctrine. They reject any further development of doctrine as well as any notion of papal infallibility. For Eastern Orthodoxy theological reflection now consists primarily of the critical activities described above. All constructive activity took place in the first seven centuries. Eastern theologians have traditionally attached little importance to the task of making Christian doctrine relevant to contemporary culture.

One notable feature of Eastern Orthodox theology is its focus on

Christian mystical experience—especially experience of God through liturgy (worship), prayer with icons (holy images), and contemplation of God's attributes. Theology is not seen so much as a way of gaining knowledge for practical or apologetic use as a path to wisdom. Within this tradition one finds very little interest in or emphasis on rational theological reflection. Spirituality absorbs theology.

The Roman Catholic Church, in contrast, holds to an ongoing process of discovery of theological truth. There is no limit to the number of possible ecumenical councils where dogmas and doctrines may be definitively pronounced. So far the church of Rome recognizes twenty-one councils as truly ecumenical and therefore authoritative. One unique aspect of Roman Catholic theology is its "magisterium," which includes the Sacred Congregation for the Doctrine of the Faith, or "the Holy Office." The Sacred Congregation is what remains of the old Inquisition, and its tasks include inspecting the writings of Catholic theologians for consistency with Scripture and official tradition. It functions as an ecclesiastical supreme court. Within Catholic theology it is never difficult to tell what beliefs are considered dogma, doctrine, opinion and heresy. The Holy Office spells that out when necessary.

Catholic theology emphasizes what is known as "natural theology"—the rational discovery and explication of God's existence and being through investigation of the natural world, including human existence in it. It also explores the intricacies of revealed truth in order to construct a perfect system that harmonizes all that can be known about God through nature, experience, Scripture and tradition.

Roman Catholic theology recognizes no real development in Christian doctrinal belief. That is, contrary to some non-Catholics' opinions, no "new truths" are ever discovered. Councils and popes may, however, elevate truths already widely believed to the status of dogma, making them official and enforceable so that no Catholic theologian may openly dispute them. In modern times this has happened with two traditional Catholic beliefs—the immaculate conception of Mary and

Mary's bodily assumption into heaven.

Since Vatican II—the twenty-first ecumenical council held in Rome from 1962 to 1965—Roman Catholic theology has undergone tremendous change. Theologians of the church have sought new articulations of dogmas and doctrines so as to make them more relevant to contemporary culture and more compatible with Protestant doctrine and styles of theological reflection. In other words, Catholic theologians have revived the second activity of the second task of theology. This, in turn, has led to some serious controversy within the church.

The history of Protestant theology begins with the great Reformation of the sixteenth century. In 1517 the German Catholic monk Martin Luther sparked a theological controversy when he nailed ninety-five theses, or points for debate, to the cathedral door in Wittenberg. Over the next several decades a new, third branch of Christian theology opened up. We call this "Protestant" because it protested Roman Catholic theology's emphasis on the authority of popes and councils as well as certain common beliefs and practices of that church.

In addition to Luther, early Protestant theologians included Ulrich Zwingli and John Calvin of Switzerland, Thomas Cranmer of England, and Menno Simons of Holland. Each of these men had been Roman Catholics but turned to some Protestant mode of theological reflection. These leaders established various traditions within Protestantism. Luther, of course, founded Lutheranism. Zwingli and Calvin were the fathers of the Reformed branch (mainly Presbyterian in Britain and North America). Cranmer helped establish the Church of England's theology (known as Episcopalian in North America). Simons was an early leader of the Anabaptists, the largest body of which today is known as Mennonites.

In spite of many differences of doctrine and opinion, these branches of Protestantism have held in common (1) a rejection of tradition (pronouncements of popes and councils) as equal with the biblical witness, (2) a rejection of natural theology as any reliable guide to true knowledge of God, (3) the affirmation of every Christian believer's right to read and interpret Scripture, and (4) the affirmation of the ongoing nature of theological reflection as a collaborative effort of God's people ("reformed and always reforming").

In spite of significant differences, all three major branches of Christian theology and church life discussed so far agree on certain basics. For instance, all agree that an essential aspect of authentic Christian belief is openness to a supernatural, spiritual reality who is involved in people's lives. No theologian in any of these branches denied the reality of God's intervention through miracles; the reality of Satan, demons and angels; Christ's future visible return; or heaven and hell. That Christianity included belief in and theological exploration of a supernatural, spiritual world was a given.

In the early nineteenth century a new form of theology evolved known as "liberal" or "modernist" theology. Eastern Orthodoxy was untouched by it, but both Protestantism and Roman Catholicism were driven to strife over this new style of theological reflection that focused the critical task on evaluating and rejecting traditional beliefs and focused the constructive task on revising doctrines and making them relevant—in the sense of palatable—to contemporary culture.

One way of understanding liberal theology is to see it as collapsing the two activities of the constructive task of theology into one: the reconstruction of Christian beliefs using relevance to culture as the primary norm. Someone has defined this new approach to theology as giving "maximal acknowledgment to the claims of modernity." Modernity means modern science; critical thinking in philosophy and historical studies; liberal social and political thought; and emphasis on individual rights, dignity and freedom of thought.

Roman Catholicism used its magisterium to squelch Catholic modernism, which virtually ceased all activity until after Vatican II. Protestant theology, however, lacking any magisterium, was largely captivated by liberal theology during the late nineteenth and early twentieth centuries. Liberal Protestant theology tended to treat modern thought as a norm—if not *the norm*—of truth even in Christian theological criticism and construction. Whatever could not be believed by enlightened modern men and women was treated as obsolete at best, superstitious at worst. This included miracles, verbally inspired books, supernatural spiritual beings, and many other traditional Christian beliefs.

Liberal theologians searched for the "essence of Christianity" that would be totally immune to the ravages of modern science and philosophy. They thought they found it in a minimal core of values centered around the teachings of Jesus. With regard to categorizing beliefs, they nearly emptied the columns of dogma and doctrine and moved almost all traditional doctrines over into the opinion category. Left over for doctrine was a minimum of moral ideas almost any humanist could endorse.

H. Richard Niebuhr, a twentieth-century critic of liberal theology, quipped that because of its one-sided emphasis on a few core values such as the "fatherhood of God" and the "brotherhood of man," in liberal theology "a God without wrath brought men without sin into a kingdom without a judgment through the ministrations of a Christ without a cross."[2]

The rise of liberal theology resulted in a predictable reaction—the development of an opposing school of Protestant theology bent on recovering and protecting Christianity's "fundamentals." Fundamentalist, or conservative, theology focused almost exclusively on theology's critical task and expended all its energy on attacking liberal theology's (and sometimes Catholic theology's) distinctives. These theologians advocated separation from and militant opposition to all heresy and apostasy. And they often tended to push all Christian beliefs they considered valid into the dogma category, leaving little to doctrine and nearly nothing to opinion. Creative construction and relevant articulation were neglected if not shunned entirely by fundamentalist theologians, who were satisfied to repeat and emphasize traditional formulations of "the faith once for all delivered."

Out of these twentieth-century fires of theological controversy emerged several new types of theology determined to avoid the extremes and excesses of both liberal and fundamentalist theologians. These might best be described as "mediating theologies" that attempted to pursue the fourfold task of theology in moderate ways that would be both faithful to the biblical message and relevant to contemporary culture. Among them are Karl Barth and Emil Brunner's neo-orthodox movement, the neo-evangelicalism of E. J. Carnell, Bernard Ramm and Carl F. H. Henry, and Jürgen Moltmann's and Wolfhart Pannenberg's eschatological theologies. All of these were, in their own ways, "back to the Reformation" movements in decidedly twentieth-century dress.

Now that we have explored and explained the tasks and traditions of theology, it is time to turn to an examination of theology's sources. To carry out the tasks set before it, theology must make use of sources and tools. What are they, and how are they used?

6

The Theologian's Tools

*L*inus and Charlie Brown are conversing about life and relationships while building a sand castle. "She was so cute," Linus says mournfully. "I used to see her in Sunday school every week. I used to just sit there and stare at her. Sometimes she'd smile at me." Returning to his castle-building, the melancholy boy adds, "Now, I hear she's switched churches."

At this point Charlie Brown interrupts Linus's soliloquy. "That'll change your theology in a hurry," he declares matter-of-factly.

We can sympathize with Linus. Whether consciously or unconsciously, we are greatly influenced by the beliefs of people we know, love or respect. Yet is this sufficient? Can we construct a solid theology on the basis of what others around us say? Shouldn't our theological commitments be built on a more substantial foundation?

Of course we shouldn't base our beliefs solely on others' opinions. But how do we go about the theological task? That is, what provides a firm foundation for constructing theology? In turning our attention to this matter, we are actually raising the question about the tools of the theological trade, what theologians often call *sources* or *norms*.

Why Theology Needs Tools

Before proceeding to enumerate theology's tools, we must return to that haunting question "Why?" Why bother with correct sources or be concerned about the norms for theology? What is it about the theological task that makes use of these tools necessary?

To find the answer, we must back up and take another run at the theological enterprise itself. In chapter three we offered a definition. Christian theology, we said, involves reflecting on and articulating the beliefs about God and the world that we share as followers of Jesus Christ, and this for the sake of living as Christians to God's glory in our contemporary context. Many people assume that such reflection or articulation is a simple, straightforward matter hardly worth further discussion. Fundamental Christian beliefs, they suggest, are automatically "there"—merely a given—for Christians all quite naturally believe certain things.

In a sense this is correct. Indeed, in chapter five we argued that Christian beliefs precede theology, for one aspect of theology is critical reflection on beliefs that we might characterize as "pretheological." Yet beliefs—even these pretheological beliefs—are not merely a given. They arise from somewhere, not nowhere. For this reason we can and must talk about the sources of theology.

"Well, okay," you might be tempted to respond; "so our beliefs come from somewhere. But perhaps they arise from that 'somewhere' in a simple manner. Maybe they come to us through simple—even blind—faith. We merely *accept* our beliefs." We all know people who believe what they do merely because their church teaches it. But as Christians we are taught to think for ourselves rather than simply taking someone else's word for it (see, for example, Acts 17:11).

One may counter with a seemingly cogent response: "So why not simply appeal to the Bible? After all, we're supposed to believe what we read in Scripture. As the old dictum says, 'God says it; I believe it; that settles it.' *If* we need theology, the only theology we need is the theology taught in the Bible (or by the church)."

The Bible is, of course, foundational. Nevertheless, it would be a mistake to close off the conversation at this premature point. We must look closer at this matter of where our theology comes from, because theology is more than merely seeking to extrapolate from the Bible a set of timeless beliefs that can be listed in rapid-fire order. Nor is the theological task complete once we have recited a church creed or confession of faith.

Another objection might be raised at this point: "Yes, creeds are not be-alls and end-alls. But what about the Bible? Surely we can go to Scripture and pull together the one true set of beliefs."

At least two difficulties make this proposal problematic. The first has to with what Scripture is. Rather than being a treatise on theology, the Bible is a beautifully rich and variegated book. Contrary to what we sometimes assume, the Bible contains neither long expositions on doctrine nor any detailed summary of the belief system of God's people. Instead we find in its pages lengthy narratives, poetry, proverbial sayings, prophetic oracles and instructions to specific groups of believers.

We are not saying that there is no theology in the Bible. On the contrary, an understanding of God and God's dealings with creation permeates its pages. A vision of who God is and what God is doing drives both the story and the admonitions found in the biblical documents. But we must keep in mind that this vision often lies beneath the surface. It is sometimes illustrated rather than explicitly stated. And it is nowhere presented in the systematic manner found in church creeds.

The second difficulty has to do with who we are. Contrary to what we sometimes assume, we are not neutral readers of Scripture. We cannot read the Bible through eyes unaffected by our own historical and cultural context.

Recently I (Stan) was leading a discussion in an adult Sunday-school class on the role of women in the church. After a session focusing on whether women should serve in church leadership positions, a man came to me. "Professor," he said, "isn't the matter really quite simple? Paul declares that an elder must be the husband of one wife. Obviously God intends that only men serve in church leadership, for only men can be husbands."

This church member didn't realize that he had read his own cultural situation into Paul's statement. He had transported Paul into our contemporary scene. In the ensuing conversation I pointed out that were our conversation taking place in Africa, we would likely be drawing a quite different conclusion from the text. As Africans we might be just as convinced that Paul is instructing us to bar polygamists from serving in church leadership. This is a blatant example of a cultural reading of Scripture. More often our use of cultural glasses is more subtle.

We can't avoid reading the Bible as the persons we are. Roger and I come to Scripture as Caucasian male evangelical Christians who have spent much of our lives in the North American Midwest (although one of us now lives on the Canadian West Coast). You come to the Bible as the person you now are, which includes where you were raised, who has influenced you and what questions you have been led to ask.

Exegetical aids can help us move out of our context as we learn more about the culture of the original recipients of the texts, but we will never be totally successful in this enterprise. Even in our attempts to understand a text through the eyes of its original readers, we remain the ones who are making the attempt, and the reading remains our reading. Our understanding of Scripture will always be filtered through the lenses of who we are and where we are in time and space.

If this is the case with our reading of Scripture, how much more must we sprinkle humility on all our theological declarations. How much more cautious must we be in drawing conclusions about the theology of the Bible. Summaries of doctrine always remain *our* summaries. Statements of biblical truth always remain *our* statements. Theological constructions are always *our* constructions and denote *our* understanding of Scripture.

Perhaps at this point you want to throw up your hands in disgust. Don't. Rather than bemoaning this situation, why not celebrate it? This situation is exactly what God intends. Rather than giving us a book of doctrine, the Holy Spirit chose to inspire the Bible as we have it—in all its diversity. And rather than crafting us as culture-free beings, the Creator chose to place us within the limitations of time and space. All this suggests that our Lord desires that we pursue theology within our own context—with all the limitations life in our context involves. This limitation may actually be what ultimately drives theology and gives it richness.

Even if this weren't the case—and even if we were able to condense the Bible into a single, complete list of timeless doctrine—this list would not mark the completion of the theological task. Theology doesn't reach its goal in a collection of truthful statements. Its goal goes beyond merely *stating* truth. We engage in theology for the purpose of *living* truth—that is, for the purpose of living *in* the truth. Therefore theology is a never-ending enterprise. We need theology not only to remind us of what we believe. We also need it to help us understand how we are to live.

Theology is not so much a science, in the modern sense of the term, as an art. Although we retain the scientist's bent toward concerted, hardheaded, even critical intellectual engagement, as theologians we are also artists. Our goal goes beyond amassing knowledge to creating a theological masterpiece. Like any work of art, our theology, while remaining intellectual in orientation, moves beyond our head to touch our heart and even our hands. For this to occur, we must use the tools of the theological trade.

The Tools of Theology

Let's preface our search for the theologian's tools by exploring how these tools function. Indeed, they fulfill two basic functions, each of which yields a more precise term for our more general designation, *tools.*

As we already noted in passing, the tools we use provide the resources for our theological construction. With a view toward this role, many theologians speak about the sources for theology. They suggest that we construct our theology from certain raw materials. In the modern era theologians differed as to whether these fundamental materials consisted of God's self-disclosure in nature and the Bible, church tradition, or the human religious consciousness. Despite such differences, they—like the classical thinkers before them—agreed that we construct theology on the basis of certain sources, whatever they may be.

The theologian's tools function in another manner as well. In addition to providing the raw data of theology, they determine the design or shape of the theology being constructed. Hence they operate as theological norms. But their function as norms is even stronger. These tools not only mold our theology, they indicate the shape our theology ought to take. They become normative for theology.

The proper tools—the sources of and norms for our theological construction—consist of the biblical message, the theological heritage of the church and the thought-forms of contemporary culture. We may say that theology arises through the interplay of these three tools. While all three are necessary, they are not all equal. Therefore we must prioritize our theological tools.

The Biblical Message

Scripture is our primary tool. This assertion probably comes as no surprise, because Christians are a "people of the book." We have always sought to be a "biblical" community, a people whose lives are based on what is written in Scripture. Nearly all Christian churches today take seriously the great Reformation hallmark, *sola scriptura* ("Scripture alone"). Thus we do not need to "prove" the Bible so as to establish its role in theology. Because the Bible is the universally acknowledged book of the Christian church—the foundational document of the faith community—it is the norm for our theological reflections.

To say the Bible is our primary tool is one thing. To see how the Bible functions as the source for theology is another matter. What is it about Scripture that exercises a norming function in our theologizing? *Everything* about the Bible is foundational to theology. To understand this, we must keep before us what Scripture is: inscripturated revelation.

Revelation is God's act of disclosing to us who he is and what he is doing. God's complete self-disclosure will come only at the end of the age. Only then will we see Christ "as he is" (1 Jn 3:2). Only then will God have brought history to its grand climax. Nevertheless, throughout history God has revealed—and is revealing—the divine nature and divine intentions.

Although at work everywhere, God has chosen to focus the divine efforts. In ancient times God worked with Israel, for this nation was to play a special role in history. Since the coming of Jesus, God has concentrated the divine work primarily through the church. Scripture informs us about these matters, or *reveals* them to us. The Bible indicates how God entered into a special relationship, or covenant, first with Israel and later with the church. And it shows how the Holy Spirit led the ancient faith communities to respond to this special relationship. Lying at the heart of the Bible is the story of Jesus the Christ, who is the fulfillment of what God had begun to do in the Old Testament era. The New Testament narrates the grand events surrounding Christ's coming, especially Jesus' ministry, death and resurrection, as well as the expansion of the early church under the direction of the Holy Spirit. The New Testament likewise presents certain of the implications the early Christian leaders (Paul, John and others) drew from these events. This biblical message—which we call "the gospel"—forms the foundation for Christian theology.

The goal of theology is to help us be the believing people of God in the world today. We are not just any people. Theology assists us in being Christ's community in a manner consistent with the way the early believers attempted to be faithful to God in their day. In this task theology turns to the biblical message.

Theology directs us to the narrative that weaves its way through the pages of the Bible. The story of God's activity in Christ reconciling us to himself provides the primary categories whereby we understand our own lives. Like the early Christians, we too have met Christ and therefore have passed from the "old life" to the "new." And as the present embodiment of the one people of God, we see the entire story of God at work in the history of Israel and the early church as our story as well.

Theology also directs us to the so-called didactic, or instructive, parts of Scripture. Theology explores this material with an eye toward Christian living in the present. In the theological enterprise, we seek to bring biblical insight to the central faith questions in the contemporary world: What does it mean to be the community of those who confess faith in the God revealed in Jesus of Nazareth? And how are we to verbalize and embody that confession in the contemporary context?

In short, theology asks, "What must we be, say and do?" And the primary tool we use in answering this question is the biblical message. We engage in theology on the basis of what we hear the apostles and prophets saying about who God is, what God has said and done, and what God intends yet to do. We look as well to what the early faith communities thought and did, conscious that they too were the people of God; indeed, they were the foundational communities of faith. Thus the Scriptures are foundational to all we do in theology. The Bible is the "informing" and the "forming" canon (standard) for the people of God throughout the generations. Or as the older theologians put it, Scripture is the "norming norm" for theology.

We might understand this foundational role of Scripture by considering the role played by the constitution of a modern democracy such as the United States. What lies at the basis of this country: is it merely a conglomerate of the fifty states? And what makes a certain people citizens of the United States of America: is it merely because they happen to live within its borders, or because they pay taxes to its government? No! The nationhood of and citizenship in the United States are somehow connected to the U.S. Constitution. This document—that is, the vision of human government expressed through it— is for the American people the agreed-upon standard for life together (at least in its political or legal dimension). The document serves both as the foundation of the structure of our community life and the final court of appeal for matters relating to that life. Therefore, to be an American means to agree to follow—or place oneself under the authority of—the Constitution. As a result, it would seem almost self-contradictory to say, "I am a good American, but I have no time for the Constitution."

In a much greater manner, the Bible—that is, the vision of what it means to be God's people expressed through Scripture—provides the foundation for our lives as Christians. It is both the *source* for understanding ourselves as God's people and the *norm* that informs us as to what we should believe and how we should live. The Bible therefore is indispensable to theology. Whatever else it may be, our theology had better be biblical.

The Theological Heritage of the Church

Heritage is our secondary tool. Many Christians see little benefit in looking at anything that happened more than a few years before they were born. Perhaps we can see ourselves in Charlie Brown's sister, Sally, as she works on her homework. Her assignment is to write an essay entitled "Church History." Putting the title on paper comes easy for Sally, but then she is stuck as to what to say about the topic. Suddenly she gets a burst of inspiration. "When writing about church history," she begins, "we have to go back to the very beginning." Now obviously on a roll, Sally continues, "Our pastor was born in 1930."

Why should we be interested in anything that happened prior to 1930? Why be concerned about a heritage that spans two millennia? One answer seems almost self-evident. It would be both foolish and impossible for us to try to jump immediately from the ancient apostles and prophets to the present context without giving any consideration to the intervening time. Indeed, we are not the first generation since the early church to seek to be the community of Christ in the world. On the contrary, we are the contemporary embodiment of a historical "trajectory," the people of God throughout the ages.

The church—from the patristic era to the present—has continually sought to express its faith. Our forebears grappled with the significance of the biblical message just as we do. Their deliberations, conclusions and confessions provide us with a lasting legacy. They have bequeathed to us a great heritage that becomes a tool for us as we, like they, engage in the theological task.

Acknowledging this heritage may come quite easily. More difficult, however, is understanding how "heritage" can be a tool in the theologian's craft, how it functions as a source and a norm for theology. Perhaps we may understand this dynamic by speaking of the theological heritage of the church as a reference point or a signpost that provides guidance in the construction of theology.

Our heritage is a reference point in that it contains examples of previous attempts to fulfill the theological mandate from which we today can learn. Looking at the past alerts us to some of the pitfalls we should avoid, some of the land mines that could trip us up, and some of the cul-de-sacs or blind alleys that are not worth our exploration. For example, theological history can warn us of possible dangers in constructing our doctrine of Christ. When Christianity came to prominence in the Roman Empire, theologians began to focus on Christ as the divine, heavenly ruler. They tried to model him after the earthly Roman emperor. As a result, their Christology emphasized a distant, exalted, wholly divine Lord far removed from the world of human existence. They lost sight of the incarnate One who shared fully in our humanness, even our human limitations. As this occurred, Christians looked more and more to Mary, rather than to Jesus, as the one who understood them and could sympathize with them. Tragically, for some medieval Christians Mary almost wholly replaced her Son as the mediator to whom people prayed.

In addition to warning us of possible dangers, past theological statements can point us in directions that hold promise as we engage in the theological calling. Contemporary attempts to revitalize the doctrine of the Trinity, for example, have gained valuable insight from the ancient Greek thinkers such as the Cappadocian fathers Basil, his brother Gregory and their friend Gregory.

Our heritage serves as a reference point in another way as well. Today we engage in theology conscious that we are members of a community of faith that spans the centuries. Because we participate in the one church of Jesus Christ, we desire to be in fellowship with all the people of God. One aspect of this true ecumenism is our attempt to retain continuity of basic doctrine with the church throughout the ages. An important way of doing this lies in paying attention to those doctrinal formulations that have gained broad acknowledgment among Christians of many generations. Such formulations have withstood the test of time and have become classic statements of theological truth, standing as milestones in the history of the church. These confessions of faith have bound the people of God together throughout the centuries. They have acted as markers indicating the boundaries of what the church has considered to be orthodox.

For example, throughout the ages the church has proclaimed that Jesus Christ is fully divine and fully human. To be truly Christian, our response to the question "Who is Jesus?" must likewise affirm these two aspects of his person. By reminding us of this, our common heritage fulfills a critical role in our quest to be the contemporary embodiment of the one people of God. And when a door-to-door evangelist claims that Christ is not the eternal Son coequal with the Father, we know that we are dealing with someone who stands outside the central current of the one church.

This does not mean that we give creeds and confessions of faith binding authority. Nor dare we set church tradition on an equal plane alongside Scripture as authoritative revelation. As our primary source or norming norm, the Bible must always stand in judgment over doctrinal formulations. And doctrinal statements should not be invoked merely for their own sake. The purpose of using the tool of heritage is to connect us with the church of all ages as we seek to construct an orthodox Christian theology in the contemporary situation.

Our earlier analogy drawn from the United States governmental system may help to clarify this. Over the centuries since the framing of the Constitution, U.S. courts have applied the vision of that document to many cases. Certain of these are landmark decisions that set precedents about the meaning of the Constitution. Contemporary judges willingly look to—even appeal to—these decisions in their own deliberations. Yet regardless of how monumental it may be, no such precedent carries the same weight as the Constitution itself. In fact, it is possible for a judge—especially on the Supreme Court—to rule in a manner that appears to overturn an earlier precedent.

In a similar manner, we look to the milestones in our heritage for guidance in our task of constructing a theology for our day. In short, in addition to being "biblical," our theology must always remain "Christian."

The Thought-Forms of Contemporary Culture

We have determined that our task is to construct a theology that is fully biblical and completely Christian, but one element still remains. Our goal is to articulate our fundamental beliefs about God and the world for the sake of living as Christians in our contemporary context. Thus we must add one additional tool: culture.

Christians have always sought to articulate their faith within the context in which God calls them to live and minister. We share the same task. Like our forebears, we desire to set forth our beliefs in a manner that will assist us in being the people of God in our world. That is, we desire a theology that is not only biblical and Christian but also relevant. A truly relevant theology embodies at least three aspects.

First, a relevant theology articulates Christian beliefs in a manner that people can understand. Every society is characterized by a particular set of cognitive tools—language, concepts, symbols and thought-forms—by means of which they view and speak about their world. The task of the church in each society is to set forth the gospel in a manner that people can understand. Theology seeks to assist the church in this mission. In our theologizing, therefore, we borrow the "language" of contemporary culture. We take seriously the way people today think. We draw from the cognitive tools of today's world so that we may express Christian beliefs in an understandable—that is, relevant—manner.

Recently I (Stan) spoke to a church gathering about the role of theology in assisting the church in proclaiming the gospel in the language of people around us, who often take their cues more from the popular media, especially television programming, than from the biblical stories. In the question-answer session, a prominent leader in the congregation objected to my thesis. "All we need to do," he said, "is to proclaim the message of the Lamb of God like the early disciples did."

This church leader was right if our intent is all we have in view, but we ought not to forget that the packaging is important as well. If we were to stand on the street corner in our multiethnic, multicultural cities and parrot John's declaration, "Behold the Lamb of God who takes away the sins of the world," the majority of passersby would not have a clue about what we were saying.

Theology seeks to assist the people of God in a type of translation task. We attempt to set forth Christian beliefs in language that people today can understand. Theology asks, "What concepts in contemporary culture form appropriate vehicles to express the biblical truth that the church has always sought to pass from generation to generation and from location to location?" This concern is not new. Throughout its history the church has looked to the categories of society for the concepts in which to express its faith commitment. To cite one classic example, when the early ecumenical councils asserted the full deity and full humanity of Christ, theologians borrowed their categories from Greek philosophy.

Second, a relevant theology speaks to the problems, longings and ethos of contemporary culture. The social context in which we live presses upon us certain specific issues, which at their core are theological. We avoid grappling with these only to our peril. How can we conceive of setting forth the faith of the Christian community without taking seriously questions about male-female relations in the light of the contemporary feminist impulse? How can we declare our beliefs without interacting with questions surrounding death in the context of the emerging influence of reincarnation or monism? How helpful are theological systems that don't tackle questions of Christ's uniqueness in the midst of the pluralism of our day?

We are not suggesting that society sets the agenda for theology or the church. Indeed, theology ought to do more in the way of setting the agenda for society. At its best, however, theology does seek to respond to the perceived needs and questions posed by people around us.

Third, a relevant theology also takes seriously contemporary discoveries and insights of the various disciplines of human learning. All truth is God's truth, which means that in engaging in theology we need not (should we say "dare not"?) limit our focus to Scripture and our theological heritage, even though they must always remain our primary and secondary sources. Our articulation of Christian belief can draw from the "secular" body of knowledge, knowing that no true knowledge is in fact ultimately secular.

Contemporary theories about addictions and addictive behavior, for example, provide valuable insights for understanding the Christian conception of sin. Likewise, current discoveries about the process of human identity formation assist us in articulating the gospel message about a new identity the Holy Spirit seeks to create in us through our union with Christ.

You may be thinking that this sounds an awful lot like syncretism. Are we advocating that we blend the Christian faith with what is fashionable today? Or worse yet, are we jettisoning the Bible in favor of mere human learning? No! We are not elevating culture above either the biblical message or our theological heritage. Nor are we proposing that contemporary thinking about religion and morals should sit in judgment over Christian teaching on these matters. Indeed, we must be constantly vigilant not to allow human learning to displace Scripture and heritage. In fact, at every turn of the road we must view—sometimes even critique—the natural and human sciences through the lenses of Christian commitment.

Despite the suggestions of some, we cannot withdraw from our social and historical context. We cannot find some supposedly culture-free realm in which only the "language of Zion"—the pure, untainted discourse of heaven—is spoken. In the end, Zion's language is the language of the day, because the Word of God always comes to expression through human categories.

The theological art involves an interplay among three tools, which in their differing ways function as sources and norms: the Bible message, the theological heritage of the church and contemporary culture. We have discussed these three tools in isolation from each other, but they are in fact inseparable. We do not first get our understanding of the Bible straight, then look to our common heritage to make sure we are orthodox, before finally seeking to talk about these matters in our social context. Rather, we draw from all three simultaneously. We read the Bible through eyes conditioned by our culture. And we read it as those who stand at this specific point in the twisting and turning trajectory of theological history.

Is this unfortunate? Quite the contrary! This is exactly how God wills that we engage in the theological task. Our Lord calls us to reflect on and to articulate the one faith of the people of God within and to the social context in which God has placed us.

Who needs theology? The contemporary church does. Why? So that we can indeed be God's people in our world. What kind of theology do we need? One that is truly scriptural, completely Christian and totally relevant. One that embodies the biblical message as proclaimed by the one people of God in a manner that interfaces with life in our specific context. Only this kind of a theology can provide us the intellectual resources we need to live out our calling as Christ's disciples in our world.

7

Constructing
Theology in Context

*I*n an installment of the comic strip *Peanuts,* Peppermint Patty is leaning against a tree, her arms folded across her stomach and her legs crossed. She is obviously enjoying her school vacation. Suddenly her best friend, Marcie, arrives on the scene.

"I signed up for a summer reading program at the library," Marcie proudly announces.

Although startled by this ominous turn of events, Peppermint Patty doesn't lose her composure. Instead she responds quite matter-of-factly, "God didn't make the summer for you to sit in the library, Marcie."

The arrow obviously finds its target, for Marcie quickly joins her friend. "You know more about theology than I thought, sir," she comments.

Like Peppermint Patty, we all know more about theology than we think we do. In fact, each of us has already gained much experience in theology, because we engage in the theological enterprise all the time, whether it be on the lay, ministerial or professional level. The question, therefore, isn't "Am I a theologian?" Rather, we must ask, "Am I a *good* theologian? Is my operative theology a *good* theology?"

We have already looked at some of the elements that go into the making of a good theology. Now we must draw these aspects together by asking, "How do I go about the theological task?" Answering this question requires that we get clear in our minds what we are seeking to accomplish. Therefore, we must look again at the nature of the theological enterprise, but this time with a view toward how we should be engaging in it.

What Kind of Constructive Theology Do We Need?

In chapter five we spoke about the two tasks of theology, the critical and constructive roles it plays in the church. Let us now recall the definition of the constructive task we offered there: *Theology's constructive task is to set forth the unity and coherence of the biblical teaching about God, ourselves and the world in the context in which God calls us to be disciples.* This definition indicates the kind of theology we need.

A biblically constructive theology. As our definition suggests, a central goal of theology is constructive. Our job as theologians is to articulate the Christian belief system, to set forth what we believe about God, ourselves and our world. Hence, theology involves "doctrine."

Lying behind the theological task is the assumption that we can bring together seemingly diverse biblical conceptions, descriptions and ideas—that we can draw together our Christian belief system into a coherent whole. Is this really possible? Can we bring quite different— if not apparently irreconcilable—statements together, or is the construction of doctrine merely a pipe dream?

Recall the mathematical analogy we borrowed in chapter five: On the surface, the addition problem $1/2 + 1/3 + 1/10 + 1/15$ appears unsolvable. The mathematician, however, knows that these fractions are not as disparate as they seem. Finding their least common denominator allows us to translate the problem into the formula $^{15}/_{30} + {}^{10}/_{30} + {}^{3}/_{30} + {}^{2}/_{30}$. This yields the sum $^{30}/_{30}$, which is 1.

In a somewhat similar manner, as theologians we seek to pierce through seemingly unsolvable theological problems. Good theology shows the connections between apparently irreconcilable theological descriptions and brings them together into a unified whole. It was this quest for a unified theology that led to some of the great theological breakthroughs in church history.

Again, let us use the doctrine of the Trinity as an example. This doctrine is nowhere explicitly taught in the Bible. (We once thought that John had given us a surefire proof text [1 Jn 5:7-8], but modern textual discoveries have shown that these verses contain an early scribal addition to John's original text.) At the same time, the God presented in the Bible is quite "complicated." The central teaching of the Old Testament is that there is only one God, the God of Israel. Yet the early believers were convinced of Jesus' deity as the unique Son of the One he called "Father" and the Lord of all. The early Christians were likewise aware that God was present within their community—through the Holy Spirit.

How could Christians bring these seemingly irreconcilable descriptions together? Specifically, how can Father, Son and Holy Spirit be one God? This question has baffled the greatest theological minds of the church through the years. But already in the third century Christian theologians came to the simple yet profound answer. The one God is Father, Son and Holy Spirit, and these three are *one* God. This awareness gave birth to the doctrine of the Trinity. It arose as an attempt to bring together the biblical revelation about the God who is one as the Father, Son and Spirit. Over the centuries Christians have agreed that this doctrine provides the only way to make sense of the biblical revelation about God.

Thus we can see that the constructive task of theology is related to the biblical message. Because our goal is to set forth Christian doctrine in a manner that brings together the seemingly diverse, even disparate, threads of the Bible, our theology must be biblically constructive. Yet while necessarily biblical, theology is never simply the juxtaposing of various scriptural statements. As is evident in the doctrine of the Trinity, theology seeks to show the connectedness of such statements.

A contextually constructive theology. We must add an even more radical qualifier: While necessarily biblical, theology is also never the product of Scripture alone. The goal of theological construction is not merely to say *what* the Bible says. Rather, our task is to construct biblical truth in a specific context. This leads us to an additional feature of the theology we need: Our theology must be contextually constructive.

We can see the need for constructing biblical truth in a specific context by returning to our illustration. The efforts of Christian thinkers to make sense of the biblical revelation about God resulted in the doctrine of the Trinity. This doctrine, therefore, reflects the biblical message. Yet the theologians who articulated the doctrine in its classic form were not living in the biblical era. Their goal was not to get back into the ancient world; they wanted to speak to their own context. Consequently, rather than limiting themselves to actual biblical language, they quite naturally borrowed the concepts and language of their culture.

The central theological question these theologians tackled was itself quite suited for their context. It focused on the apparent "mathematical" puzzle, "How can God be both 'one' and 'three' at the same time?" Their answer was simple enough: God is not one in the same way that he is three. But to present this simple answer they needed to delve deeper: Exactly in what sense is God one, and in what sense is he three? To explain, thinkers drew from the categories of their day. Latin Christian thinkers spoke of God as one *substantia* (substance) and three *personae* (persons). Later the Greek theologians declared God is one *ousia* (essence) but three *hypostaseis* (centers of consciousness).

By using these terms, the church theologians had obviously moved beyond biblical categories. They drew instead from the philosophical language of their day. In so doing, they "contextualized" the biblical message. They sought to understand the scriptural witness to God in a manner that made sense in their world. This ought not to surprise us. Indeed, how could it be otherwise?

Obviously, we don't inhabit the ancient world. Nor do we live in the first century, in the era of the early church. I might long to return to that age, "to walk today where Jesus walked" and thereby "feel him close to me," but no one can do so. We cannot literally jump back into the first-century world or its culture; nor is it God's intent to place us back in that context. Rather, our Lord desires that we speak and live as disciples in the world in which he has placed us. This truth has far-reaching implications for theology. It suggests that our task is not simply to repeat the theological declarations of any previous era, even the biblical era. We don't simply lift statements out of Joshua, Jeremiah, John and James, thinking this is the end of theology. Rather, we seek to understand the revelation of God mediated through the biblical writers for *our* context and *our* world. Indeed, try as we will, there is no alternative. We can't avoid living in the contemporary context; we can't shed the thought-forms, concepts, questions and aspirations of our world.

To cite an obvious example, in a sense none of us who live in the so-called English-speaking world actually speak English. Rather, we all speak the form of English spoken by people around us—people in our time and locale. Few of us address others in the language of Shakespeare. Differences in word meanings often make for humorous and sometimes serious misunderstandings between English speakers from different parts of the world.

The same point is true for the language of faith. Not many among us are old enough to resonate with the ethos embodied in the words of Philip Bliss's nineteenth-century hymn:

Brightly beams our Father's mercy
From His lighthouse evermore,

But to us He gives the keeping
Of the lights along the shore.[1]

Just as we can't avoid living in the contemporary context, we can't avoid bringing this context into our theologizing. And why would we want to, if our goal is to construct Christian belief for the sake of being Christ's disciples today?

There is no such thing as a culturally disembodied theology. We cannot do otherwise than to read and interpret the Bible—that is, to seek to understand the biblical message—within the context in which we are living. The question, therefore, is not "Should we construct a contextualized theology?" Rather, we must ask ourselves, "Are we good contextual theologians?" That is, are we constructing a theology that expresses what the Bible says in a manner that can speak to our world? In short, constructive theology is by its very nature contextual.

Sound familiar? Indeed, this admonition ought to draw us back to chapter six, to the discussion of the tools we employ in the theological craft. We'll take another run at this, viewing it, however, from a different angle.

How Do We Contextualize Theology?

We have defined Christian theology as the articulation of the fundamental beliefs about God and the world that we share as followers of Jesus Christ, and this for the sake of living as Christians in our contemporary context. From this we concluded that the theology we construct must be truly scriptural, completely Christian and totally relevant. It must embody the message of the Bible as proclaimed by the one people of God throughout history in a manner that interfaces with life in our world.

How do we go about doing this? Where do we begin? What provides the jumping-off point for this process? Although some Christians might suggest that we simply accept the historical teachings of the church, for believers interested in contextualizing theology, two other alternatives arise immediately: move from the Bible to culture, or move from culture to the Bible.

Should we start with the Bible? The answer to "Where do we begin?" can only be "With the Bible." Indeed, the Bible-centered method seems correct. After all, as theologians we should always begin with Scripture. But how do we begin with the Bible? The answer may appear obvious: Beginning with the Bible means focusing our theologizing toward the goal of discovering the system of doctrine found in its pages.

Our theology must embody the biblical message, which is the norming norm of our theology. But as we have already indicated, the search for the one biblical system of doctrine is a mirage. Consider this: What do we find when we read the Bible? A book of doctrine, a discourse outlining one single, timeless doctrinal system? Hardly! Scripture consists of narratives, pithy sayings, poetic reflections. Even the teaching sections, such as Paul's letters, while not devoid of doctrinal content, are more concerned with applying belief to life than with providing a lengthy exposé of Christian doctrine. And what is our ultimate goal in reading Scripture? It is not to escape out of our context so as to get back into the biblical world. Instead, we seek to express Christian doctrine in the categories of the world in which we live.

Hence, the discovery of some supposedly biblical system of doctrine is too precise. It cannot be what we mean by "beginning with the Bible." Perhaps a bit looser answer will fit the bill. Maybe beginning with the Bible means focusing our energies on discovering what issues the Scriptures themselves raise as well as on how the biblical authors respond to them.

This approach holds promise. Indeed, the Bible announces and addresses the central theological questions about God, ourselves and the world. We come to Scripture because we want to know who the Bible says God is, what God's intentions for creation are, and how we fit into God's plans. We are likewise interested in the biblical diagnosis of the human condition, as well as God's remedy for it. And we want to understand what it means to live as Christians. In short, we want the Bible to set our theological agenda, and we want our doctrinal constructions to be faithful to the Bible's message.

At this point, you might be tempted to say, "This seems to be the answer to our question. We have finally found the key to deducing a truly biblical theology." But before we rush to embrace the Bible-centered approach as we have articulated it—before we announce the successful conclusion of the discussion and publish our findings—we ought to take another look.

Going to the Bible first is a helpful proposal, yet it poses one grave danger. In our quest to read and be faithful to Scripture, we may overlook our culture. We may not give sufficient attention to the questions people today are asking. As a result, our doctrine—as biblical as it may appear to be—may in the end be irrelevant to the world in which God calls us to live as disciples. In short, our attempt to construct a *biblical* theology may short-circuit our attempt to construct a biblical *theology*. This was the problem with simply preaching "the Lamb of God," as we discussed in chapter six. Few people today are asking, "Where can I find the perfect sacrifice for sins?"—which is the question the message of the Lamb of God is designed to answer. (They are, however, asking questions related to how sin can be overcome, and we will cover this later.)

Should we start with culture? The danger posed by the Bible-centered approach suggests a second possible beginning point—our culture. What would a culture-centered approach to theology look like? Simply stated, beginning with culture means seeking to hear the spiritual cries of the contemporary world. We do this in many ways: by observing people around us, listening to their conversations, keeping up with the news, becoming aware of cultural expressions of a deeper spiritual quest, following intellectual developments, and even studying philosophy. We observe and listen so as to discern the questions and concerns of contemporary men and women. Having discovered these, we go back to the Bible for a response. We take our culture with us to the texts. We read the Scriptures asking, "How does the Bible provide answers to the questions people today are raising?"

For such a scriptural rationale for this endeavor we need look no further than Jesus' own model. Repeatedly our Lord tailored his message to meet the needs of his audiences. He allowed his awareness of their questions to shape his response. Consider, for example, how differently Jesus articulated the gospel to the Samaritan woman (Jn 4:1-26) than to Nicodemus (Jn 3:1-21). He spoke to her in categories arising from her life and religious context—living water, the proper way of worship, the coming Messiah. But to Nicodemus, our Lord talked about things the prominent Jewish teacher should have known—spiritual birth, the Son of Man. In each case, Jesus perceived the inner questions, struggles and spiritual aspirations of the person he was addressing. He knew the categories with which they thought and viewed life. He then presented his message as the answer to their quest in a manner they could understand.

Having said all this, we must quickly add a caution. We don't want to rush headlong into the culture-first approach, for it too poses a grave danger. It can lead us into the error of giving too much weight to the questions and concerns of contemporary men and women. Doing so bears three potential difficulties.

First, focusing too closely on our culture may lead us to take our theological agenda from our world rather than from the Bible. We may thereby overlook those biblical insights that don't seem to address specifically the questions our contemporaries are asking. Indeed, the Bible may offer a cure for ills that people don't realize they have. Second, the focus on culture may blind us to places where our society and the Bible are at odds. We may fail to bring a thoroughly biblical critique to our culture. Third, focusing on culture may lead us to allow our world to determine the content of theology. We may fall into the trap of "cultural accommodation." In the attempt to be relevant we may lose the gospel.

Take the biblical concept of sin as an example. We ought to speak of sin in culturally sensitive ways. Hence, we might draw on findings in psychology to speak about the addictive aspect of sin. Or we may borrow the language of "failure." Making such connections facilitates us in articulating a culturally constructive theology. But we dare not buy into the trend to jettison the concept of personal responsibility and accountability. If we excuse culpable conduct because the perpetrators were themselves "victims," we are no longer talking about what the Bible calls "sin." We have lost the gospel.

A truly relevant Christian theology always returns to the Bible as the norming norm. It seeks to maintain the gospel, even as it articulates Christian beliefs by means of contemporary language and with a concern for contemporary questions. While we must always draw the *content* of our beliefs from the Bible, we dare not forget that their *form* must arise from the questions and concerns of contemporary men and women. Otherwise people today simply will not be able to understand our message. The form of Christian teaching must vary from age to age and culture to culture; yet the content will always be the same—the biblical truth that "Jesus is the answer."

Let's start with a "trialogue." Each of the two alternatives we explored has great merit. But when taken alone, each has serious weaknesses and hidden dangers. Therefore, we can't opt for either approach by itself. Affirming that both are correct yet neither is the answer leaves us in a quandary: How do we construct a contextual theology? Our answer is: By bringing our understanding of Scripture, our cognizance of our heritage and our reading of our cultural context into a creative trialogue.

Without realizing it, this is the way we normally engage in theology. We sometimes think we can operate according to one or the other of the alternatives noted above. We often assume that we can view our culture as objective observers, deciphering the questions and aspirations of people around us with their spiritual quest in view, then returning to the Bible to find the answers. Or, more often, we think we can read the Bible through culturally neutral eyes. We believe that we can stand in the place of the original readers—ancient Israel, the Corinthian believers, the church in Ephesus—and know almost instinctively what the text means. And having come to determine this one universal objective meaning, we believe we are in a place to tell everybody we meet, "Thus saith the Lord!" or "My Bible says!"

The fact is, however, our understanding of Scripture and our reading of culture are interrelated, and both are affected by our place in the ongoing movement of God's people in the world. Rather than bemoaning this inevitable situation, why not see it as the key to creative theology that it represents?

To see how the trialogue—the interaction among Bible, heritage and culture—provides theology with a creative edge, let's look at the history of the doctrine of the atonement—that is, at how theologians have understood Jesus' mission on behalf of sinful humans.

Beginning in the late second century, Christian thinkers generally viewed Jesus' work as a great victory over Satan. This *ransom theory* declared that our sin had brought us into bondage to the devil. If we are to go free, God must buy us back by means of a ransom to which the devil would also consent. Jesus was this ransom. When Satan slew the sinless Christ, he took something that did not belong to him. Justice demanded that he release those who were in bondage to him.

By the eleventh century the ransom theory had lost its persuasive power. European society had changed, and the older view was out of sync with the new feudal order. In keeping with the understandings of feudal society, Anselm proposed what we call the *satisfaction theory*. He pictured humans as feudal barons, God's vassals, who have refused to give God the honor due him as their Sovereign. Through his death, however, Jesus satisfied God's honor on behalf of humankind. Rather than a ransom paid to the devil, therefore, in Anselm's theory Christ's death was directed toward God.

Eventually the feudal order was replaced by nations and national governments. To meet the challenge of speaking in the new social context, the satisfaction theory needed a thorough overhaul. What resulted was the *penal-substitution theory*. This view teaches that rather than an affront to God's honor, our sin transgresses divine law. Hence we are not rebellious vassals of the divine king but criminals, guilty of crimes against the divine government. Into this courtroom drama stepped Jesus. He paid the penalty for our transgressions at the bar of divine justice.

Repeatedly in theological history one additional understanding of Jesus' work has appeared, the *moral-influence theory.* Rather than effecting some great transaction in God, the cross woos our hearts. Jesus' death is the grand exhibition of God's great love for us, which frees us from our fear of God's wrath and kindles in us a desire to love God.

Which of these depictions is the correct statement of the doctrine? Each of us may be personally attracted to one of these theories. Perhaps one of them was even instrumental in your conversion. But our question isn't "Which of them do you *like?* Which do you *prefer?*" but "Which of them is *correct?*"

In the end, our question has no answer. No one theory ranks as *the* orthodox interpretation. More importantly, we can only speak about the correctness of each theory as an expression of the gospel that speaks within a specific cultural situation. The truth of each is in part determined by the context to which it seeks to bear the biblical message.

Viewed from this perspective, we might say that each of these theories presents a dimension of what remains a mystery greater than any single explanation—the mystery of salvation. We can speak about this mystery only in the context of our own lives or in the context of the questions and aspirations of specific people.

How did each of these theories arise? Did each come about solely through reading the Bible or solely through exegeting culture? No! Each of the great atonement theories was the product of a trialogue. They arose as Christian thinkers looked for a way to articulate the Christian message—"Jesus died for our sins"—in the context in which they were living. Their search for an answer to the theological question

"What is the meaning of Jesus' work on our behalf?" led them to read Scripture, heritage and culture together. The conclusions they reached indicate that they were thoroughly bathed in Scripture, completely cognizant of the christological convictions of the church throughout the ages, and keenly perceptive of the felt needs of their own culture. The history of the doctrine of the atonement offers us a great theological legacy. Conscious of this legacy, let's do likewise. Let's listen to Scripture, heritage and culture so that we might determine what it means to express the significance of Jesus' work to people in our world. And beyond this one doctrine, let's bring Scripture, heritage and culture into creative trialogue so that we can construct a helpful theology for today's needs.

How Do We Systematize Our Theology?

We have indicated that our theologizing can lead us to construct individual doctrines that bring together seemingly disparate descriptions, but we haven't yet spoken about how we can have a truly *systematic* theology. What transforms our theology from a juxtaposing of loosely related doctrines into a systematic theology for our times is an organizing theme, a scarlet thread that runs through all of Christian doctrine. Theology becomes systematic by means of what we might call its "integrative motif."

What is an integrative motif? Systematic theologians ideally order their presentation of the Christian faith around one specific concept. This concept acts as the central organizational feature of the systematic theology. It is the theme around which the various doctrines are structured.

Theological history has witnessed the devising of many integrative motifs. For example, Martin Luther's quest to find a gracious God led him to center his theologizing on the idea of "justification by faith." John Calvin, in turn, focused his theological work on "God's glory." Recent theologians have sounded various notes, including "liberation," "women's experience" and "story." But no theme has rivaled

"God's kingdom" or "the reign of God" in its ability to capture the modern ethos.

The designation itself—*"integrative* motif"—suggests what such a theme does and why it is important. An integrative motif provides the key that *integrates* the various doctrines into a single whole. This central theme provides a focus for the issues the theologian discusses, and it illumines how the theologian formulates his or her responses to these issues. In short, *an integrative motif is the central idea that provides the thematic perspective in light of which the theologian understands all other theological concepts and gives them their relative meaning or value.*

A truly helpful integrative motif performs one additional function. It provides the theological bridge that joins Bible, heritage and culture. A truly helpful central theme captures the essence of the biblical message. At the same time, it taps into the heartbeat of contemporary culture, bringing to light the heartfelt needs of people today. And in all of this, it remains true to the central thrust of the theological discussions throughout the ages.

How do we choose our integrative motif? We have already implicitly indicated how we should select an integrative motif: A candidate for our central theme must bring Bible, heritage and culture together. Our choice for the central theme of our theology must embody the heart of the biblical message, express the one faith of the church and speak to the deep, heart-felt longings of contemporary society. If these are the qualifications, the method should now be obvious: "reading" Scripture, our heritage and our culture.

We read the Bible and ask, "What is the Bible's central message for today?" We study church history and ask, "What has stood at the heart of God's work through the church as evidenced in the confessions and theologies of the past?" We listen to our culture and ask, "What spiritual longings are coming to expression today, and how are these being expressed?" When the trialogue focusing on these three questions converges, we have discovered a solid candidate around which to set forth a cogent, cohesive articulation of Christian beliefs. We have discovered a potential integrative motif for our systematic theology.

A personal illustration will shed light on this concept of the integrative motif. Our own reading of Scripture, heritage and culture has coalesced around the idea of the individual-in-relationship, that is, around the concept of "community."[2]

First, the theme of community is centrally biblical. At the heart of the entire biblical drama is the relational God at work bringing about the eternal community—a redeemed people dwelling in the renewed creation and enjoying fellowship with the triune God. Second, the theme of community is centrally Christian. The triune God (the community of Father, Son and Spirit) and the church as the fellowship (community) of Christ's followers have stood at the heart of our common theological heritage as Christians throughout the centuries. Finally, the theme of community is centrally contemporary. As modernity with its focus on radical individualism wanes, contemporary thinkers are rediscovering community. Indeed, the central goal of culture is the attempt to construct and sustain bonds of commonality among individual members of that society. Therefore community offers a promising central theme around which to understand the seemingly disparate doctrines of our faith. Let's see how these doctrines might find their unity through this concept.

Theology: The eternal God is the foundation for community, for God is none other than the social Trinity, the eternal community of Father, Son and Spirit. As the social trinity, God is indeed love.

Anthropology: God created humankind to be the "image of God." Because God is community, we are created for community, created to love and thereby show what God is like. Sadly, however, we have failed to live in love. Instead we are at enmity with God, ourselves and creation.

Christology: As the Son sent by the Father, Jesus has revealed to us who God is and who we were created to be. In Christ, God has acted to overcome our enmity and failure and to restore us to fellowship with God, each other and creation.

Pneumatology: The Holy Spirit effects in us God's design for us, which focuses on community.

Ecclesiology: Being in community means belonging to God's people, the community of Christ's disciples.

Eschatology: The fellowship we now enjoy through the Spirit is only a foretaste of what we will share in eternity. As resurrected saints dwelling in the new creation and enjoying the presence of the triune God, we will know the fullness of community.

Soon we will turn you loose. We will invite you to embark on the great adventure of constructive theology. But when you do so, keep in mind that ultimately theology is not an exercise in intellectual acumen designed to expand our minds. Its final goal is *life*.

8

Bringing Theology into Life

*F*arley, the lovable old dog in the comic strip *For Better or for Worse,* has died rescuing April. As the eventful day ends, April's father, John Patterson, comes to her bedroom to see how the little girl is coping with the tragic development. "Still awake, April?" he asks tenderly.

"Uh huh." The girl then confides, "I wish it didn't happen, Daddy."

"So do I."

April turns to her father. "It's all my fault!" she cries.

"No, it wasn't, April," John responds reassuringly. "He was a very old dog. It was Farley's time to go."

Leaning on her daddy's shoulder, the little girl pines for her dog: "I wish he would have lived forever."

"Nobody lives forever, honey," he says gently. Then the wise father tailors an explanation: "That's what makes us all so special. We are temporary. Our lives are on loan to us. Just for a while. . . . And nobody knows how long each life will be. That's why we have to take care of each other and to remember every day to appreciate the ones we love."

Comforted by these words, April falls asleep. His mission accomplished, John slips out of his daughter's room. But then what he has said hits home. Finding his wife, Elly, John envelops her in an unanticipated, unexplained hug.

This is theology at its best. Good theology is never content to remain on the theoretical level; it always affects life.

In this chapter we will explore how theology is dislodged from the realm of intellectual theory and enters the world in which we live. We will begin by clarifying the connection between theory and lived experience.

Theology and Life

Our search for a connection takes us back once again to our understanding of the nature of theology. Repeatedly we have asked, What is the theological enterprise? What are we seeking to accomplish? Now we take another run at this matter, looking at theology through the lenses of the question, What is the relationship between theory and life? Does theology stand apart from life?

On first impulse one might protest the entire idea of a connection between the two: "Theology stands above or apart from life. It belongs to the intellectual not the practical realm." Because this protest harbors a specific understanding of the goal of theology, we could take the objection even further. We could argue that theology is the quest for timeless intellectual truth, whose goal is to bring together all truth into a single, all-encompassing, coherent unity and whose purpose is to bring us to know, comprehend or even contemplate this grand system of eternal, intellectual truth. To such a line of thinking, however, we must voice an emphatic "No!" For the ultimate goal of theology is not knowledge per se.

Many Christians do, however, think of theology as the amassing of a great body of truths, or propositions, about God. Although its roots lie earlier, this view of theology paralleled the ascendancy of the modern scientific method. During the seventeenth and eighteenth centuries, which we often call the Age of Reason, thinkers developed what became the modern understanding of knowledge: We can come to know reality, because it is an objective given that we can dissect, as it were, under the scrutiny of human reason. Certain Christian thinkers, in turn, conceived of the theological enterprise in accordance with this model: The theologian is also a scientist. Like other scientists, the theologian employs reason in the pursuit of knowledge.

Viewed from this perspective, the theologian and the scientist do not differ in their method of inquiry; they follow the same basic approach. Both observe phenomena from which they gather and organize data. Both seek to deduce certain laws or principles that explain the phenomena. By collecting these conclusions, which they state in the form of assertions or propositions, both attempt to contribute to a growing body of human knowledge.

What separates the theologian from the scientist in this modern understanding is the subject matter each pursues. Whereas the scientist is interested in some aspect of the universe, the theologian is concerned with knowledge about God obtained by means of keen observation of God's self-disclosure. For Protestant theologians the primary source of this divine revelation is the Bible. For them, therefore, the goal of theology is to collect whatever true assertions about God (and God's world) can be deduced from the Scriptures.

The quest for knowledge remains undeniably a great legacy of the Enlightenment. As Christians we can applaud this aspect of the Age of Reason. We believe that because God is the Creator of the entire universe, all knowledge is ultimately from God and about God. We can also applaud the efforts of theologians to borrow the tools of the Enlightenment in an attempt to discover the truth God has given us.

We cannot, however, go all the way with the Age of Reason. Knowledge garnered through the scientific method is indeed *a* good. But it isn't *the* good. We must avoid any suggestion that the accumulation of such knowledge is the final goal of our existence. Our purpose is not to amass a wealth of knowledge for its own sake. Nor should we be under any illusion that the possession of knowledge is inherently good. This is often the error of the academic theologian.

At this point one might retort: "This may be true about knowledge the scientist gathers, but surely *biblical* knowledge is in a different category." No! Not even solid, biblically based theological knowledge—correct doctrine or the compilation of all true assertions about God—is the be-all and end-all of life. Remember that Paul adamantly sought to divest the Corinthian believers of this faulty accent: "Knowledge puffs up . . ." (1 Cor 8:1).

No one is more knowledgeable about theological things than our archenemy and his comrades. James notes that even the demons believe that there is only one God (Jas 2:19). We might say that Satan is the greatest theologian in the universe. He is cognizant of a great body of theological knowledge. But what good does it do him? The ultimate goal of theology, therefore, is not the accumulation of the facts of the Bible, as important as that task may seem.

If theology doesn't stand apart from life as the delineation of the facts of God from Scripture, then perhaps we should look elsewhere. Maybe life determines theology. Maybe we should derive our convictions from our experience. Maybe the correct movement is from life to theological reflection. To many Christians this may sound like a novel suggestion, but it is not new. Over the last two hundred years a number of theologians have closely linked theology with experience, and this approach remains quite popular today.

Should we, then, move in this direction? Again we must respond with an emphatic "No!" for experience all too easily leads to subjectivism. How often have discussions abruptly ended with one person saying, "Well, that's my experience!" Who can argue with experience?

Who can, indeed! The fact is, we often must argue with experience, for experience is not an infallible guide. What is, is not necessarily what ought to be. Nor is what we see—what we think we are experiencing—always what is true. Indeed, we have an uncanny ability to deceive or delude ourselves. Rather than trusting the "truth" of our experience, we need to apply truth *to* our experience. Truth must stand over experience, appraising, even judging, it. We must strongly object to a focus on experience, for it oversimplifies what is in fact a complex relationship, for there is no such thing as pure experience.

Some no doubt will adamantly protest our claim by pointing out, "We have experiences all the time." Of course we have experiences. But despite what we generally assume, we never have a *pure* experience—that is, experience never comes to us simply as itself. On the contrary, an event always occurs within a context. What we call "experience" is actually the blending of something that comes *to* us with something we bring to our world. And what we bring is an interpretive framework, a worldview, a way of viewing the world that forms our perception—our experience—of the world and of life. This interpretive framework is crucial to experience, for it facilitates our experiences, allowing us to experience the world as we do.

For example, while driving down a street, you notice a light ahead changing from green to yellow and then to red. What happened? What did you experience? The answer may seem obvious: "The light turned red." The obvious nature of the occurrence might make one oblivious to the point. What you experienced, even how you described the event, was based on the context you brought to it—on your presence at the wheel of the car, your awareness of the traffic rules of the land, your memory of the day you got a ticket for running a yellow light and so on. In short, we never see the world directly. Rather, we experience our world through the lenses of an interpretive framework. We know the world as persons, not as machine-like receptors.

Various factors contribute to our interpretive framework. We derive it from the society in which we participate—the way we speak (our language), the influence of people we know, the values of the social groups in which we participate (including religious groups). Our worldview arises as well from our background—the way we were brought up, the way we were socialized, what we were taught to believe. And it emerges from our past—how we've coped with life—as well as our anticipations for the future. In short, our interpretive framework develops from the manifold influences that come our way and encounters with life we have had, are having and will yet have.

Theology and life are interdependent. If you have latched on to this idea, you may now be thinking, "Doesn't this mean that our interpretive framework is always subject to change?" Exactly. But beyond this, experience and our interpretive framework are interdependent. Our worldview produces experience. (We experience life as we do because we believe what we do.) At the same time, experience leads us to reappraise—even to alter radically—our worldview. (We believe what we do because we have experienced what we have experienced.)

This is precisely what conversion is all about. Paul's encounter on the Damascus road, for example, did not occur in a vacuum. He was steeped in the Jewish faith. He knew the Old Testament. And he had already been exposed to the Christian message. He witnessed Stephen's martyrdom, for example. Paul's worldview formed the context in which he experienced the exalted Lord Jesus that day. This encounter, in turn, so jolted his "categories" that he drastically revised his belief structure: "Whatever was to my profit I now consider loss for the sake of Christ" (Phil 3:7).

Charles Colson offers a more contemporary example. At one time he supposedly remarked that if necessary he would run over his own grandmother in his quest to insure the reelection of then President Richard Nixon. But when Colson met Jesus Christ, he—like Paul—gained an entirely new outlook. Commitment to Christ resulted in this once ruthless power monger being transformed into an advocate for justice and causes such as prison reform.

Whatever it may look like, our interpretive framework comprises our fundamental belief system and constitutes our basic theology. Our belief system—our theology—therefore, stands in a reciprocal relationship to life. Theological convictions lead us to look at life the way we do and allow us to experience the world as we do. Our life experiences, in turn, bring our theological convictions into the picture and cause us to reexamine, reevaluate and even revise our convictions about God, ourselves and our world.

The interplay between theory and life goes on all the time, but because it is so much a part of who we are, we may not even be aware that it is happening. Enter the theological task! In the theological enterprise we consciously bring to light the interaction between beliefs and experiences. This includes exploring our beliefs in the light of our experiences. More importantly, it entails discovering the implications of that belief system for how we look at, live in and experience the world.

Christian theology views the world from a particular perspective. Therefore, we could alter our earlier definition of theology: *The Christian theological task is to use the tools of the craft (the biblical message, our theological heritage and contemporary culture) to construct an interpretive framework that views all reality from the perspective that God has encountered us in Jesus of Nazareth.* Our goal in engaging in this task is to see the world through "Christian" eyes. We desire to understand and experience all reality in accordance with solid Christian beliefs.

Theology is the pursuit of wisdom. A central, crucial goal of our theologizing is right thinking. As Christians we want to view the world in accordance with our conviction that Jesus is the Christ. But our desire goes further. We don't merely want to peer at the world with Christian eyes (indeed, seeing the world as a disciple would not allow us to do so); we desire to *be in the world* and to conduct ourselves in a manner that arises from, is consistent with and even lives out the Christian worldview.

This desire suggests that the final goal of theology lies deeper than intellectual commitments, as important as they are. Our task is more than merely developing a Christian belief system. In a word, this deeper goal is *wisdom*. We engage in theology so that we might attain wisdom. We can never be content to allow our theologizing to remain on the level of knowledge. We can't stop with the accumulation of propositions, as orthodox, coherent and complete as our set of doctrines may be.

Our Lord doesn't intend to be Lord of our intellectual commitments alone. He desires to transform our character and our conduct. He wants our commitment to him to take its lodging in our heart and to move our hands. Theology plays a role in this process. In fact, right belief, or correct doctrine, is vital to Christian living. We seek theological knowledge so that we might be wise Christians—those who live holy lives to the glory of God. Therefore, the true theologian explores how the great confessions of faith we recite on Sunday morning affect our Monday world.

Living as Christian Theologians

How do we engage in the kind of theologizing that connects theory with life, that brings Sunday morning into our Monday world? The place to begin is with faith. One classical definition of theology we noted earlier is "faith seeking understanding."

Since theology begins with faith, must a person be a believing, practicing Christian to be a theologian? Yes! In one sense, it is possible to construct a biblical, orthodox, contextual statement of Christian belief and not be a Christian. It is possible to explore the implications of Christian belief for our understanding of and living in the world yet not be a believer. But in the end such an enterprise does not qualify as Christian "theology." Instead we might call it "religious studies," the study of specific religious systems of belief, such as Christian doctrine.

While similar to theology, religious studies isn't theology, because the stance toward the topic is different. Scholars of religion seek to approach Christian doctrine and practice in a detached, scientific manner. They look at it "from the outside." They view it as an objective reality, a given, that they can scrutinize. Christian theologians, in contrast, are not neutral. They approach the study of Christian belief "from within," as those who believe in the God revealed in Christ and who participate in the faith community.

This doesn't mean, however, that the theologian is necessarily a person of superior faith. Assent to Christian doctrine is not faith. Faith is our personal response to God's call on our life, and this response entails an intellectual reorientation. We affirm the basic assertions embedded in the gospel (for example, Jesus died for me). But faith also involves our will and our emotions. In faith we commit ourselves to the God revealed in Jesus Christ, whom to know is to love. So theologians are not necessarily persons of greater faith, even though we would anticipate that the study of theology would lead us all to greater trust in, love for and obedience to our great God and Savior. With faith we move into life. As people of faith we seek to take Christian commitment—Christian belief—into our world. We should be viewing several dimensions of life through theological eyes.

One focus of our endeavors is our social context, our culture. Taking faith into life means looking at the society in which we live through theological eyes. In chapter seven we spoke about the role of culture in the construction of systematic theology. There we noted that we are inevitably influenced by culture. In our earlier discussion, we admonished you to listen to culture. Now we must flesh out a bit more what is involved in this listening.

First, listening involves determining what we should be listening to. It is good to listen to the various venues that provide a cultural voice, that give expression to the ethos of our day or that embody the often unexpressed inner psyche of our contemporaries. There are many such windows on our culture—literature, music, films, television programs, art, even newspapers and magazines.

As Christian theologians we should be aware of those cultural expressions that capture the imagination of people around us—those that make the headlines, that become the topic of conversations that don't blow over in a day. These cultural phenomena embody the thoughts, aspirations, dreams and quests of people around us.

Another aspect of culture worth listening to is our public or institutional life. Therefore, we should look at our culture asking what institutions shape people's lives today, what institutions command their allegiance.

Second, listening involves scrutinizing cultural phenomena. We do this by asking the right questions with the goal of teasing out the particular worldview or belief system at work in cultural phenomena. We want to bring to light the theology they embody. This, in turn, gives us a window both on what people around us believe and what beliefs are exercising a shaping and molding influence on people today. So we should be continually probing, seeking to find hints that reveal the theology underlying our cultural life. We should pose questions such as: What understanding of God, ourselves and the world is motivating this cultural expression? What does this phenomenon say about what people today believe?

Third, listening involves appraising and responding to culture. It is not sufficient simply to discover the theology at work in our culture; we must interact with it. Thus we probe further: How does this theology square with Christian conviction? To what extent is what I see here a helpful contemporary expression of biblical theology? Is the gospel present here? Or am I finding non-Christian, even antibiblical beliefs at work?

As we probe, we allow ourselves to be challenged: How does this cultural expression cause me to rethink my convictions? Have I got it wrong and therefore need to shift my belief structure at this point? But we must also challenge our culture: What do I find here that compels me to respond with an unflinching no? And how would sound Christian doctrine correct the bad theology operative here?

When placed under the scrutiny of critical theological analysis, many contemporary cultural expressions turn out to be at best a mixed bag. Take the film *Sommersby,* produced and shown in movie theaters in the early 1990s. The plot concerns a Southern plantation owner who returns from the Civil War a changed man—changed for the better. When he stands trial for a murder committed before the war, however, it comes to light that he is in fact someone else. The real Jack Sommersby died in the war. Nevertheless, the impostor Jack Sommersby goes to the gallows maintaining he is indeed the real Jack Sommersby. Why? Because publicly acknowledging who he really is would nullify all the good he has done under his assumed identity— good that has benefited the Sommersby wife and children. He dies for a lie, but in so doing he sacrifices his life for the sake of others. The film concludes with a symbolic resurrection scene: the townspeople restore their rundown church.

In a sense, this is the gospel—self-sacrifice for the sake of others. Yet it presents only a partial gospel. Jack Sommersby functions as a Christ-figure. But of course Jesus did not live and die under an assumed identity. Sommersby is also a model human: this is how we should live. But the movie fails to remind us that we cannot do so without the transforming presence of the Holy Spirit.

Another aspect of theological engagement with culture focuses on the issues of the day. As Christians we ought to be viewing grave social questions through theologically informed eyes. This involves being aware of the issues themselves. What questions, problems and decisions are we facing today? What is being discussed and debated in the newspapers and television newscasts? What topics are emerging in the political campaigns?

Our goal, however, is not merely to become aware of the key issues, but to engage them in dialogue. As with other aspects of contemporary cultural life, we seek to determine the theological dimensions of each issue. To do so, we ask certain key questions: What is at stake theologically here? What theological commitments lie beneath the surface of the various arguments we hear in the debate over this issue? What theology underlies or comes to expression in the alternatives currently offered?

In addition to discerning the theological dimensions involved, we attempt to apply Christian convictions to the situation. We ask: What aspects of Christian belief help to illuminate the deeper aspects of the problem? How might the Christian worldview point the way forward? What solutions or answers does the Christian understanding suggest?

To illustrate, consider doctor-assisted suicide. The current discussion is driven by several worldview or theological commitments. For example, proponents of doctor-assisted suicide often appeal to individual rights: "I own my life and my body. Therefore I have the right to do with myself as I please, even to decide when and how I will die." Christian theology, however, can never speak that language. Ultimately our lives are not our own; they belong to the One who created us. And we do not exist simply for ourselves, but for the sake of others. Consequently we can't view our life, or our death, as something we own or control. Life—and death—is a stewardship.

Proponents also focus attention on personal happiness: "When I find that life is no longer worth living, I will end it." But on what basis dare I conclude that my subjective sense of happiness is the final measure of the worth of life? Ultimately our lives are not valuable because we are happy, but because they are connected with a purpose greater than ourselves. In this context, even pain can have meaning—as it serves a higher purpose. Indeed, steadfastness in the midst of adversity can be an encouragement to those who are facing tragedy to place their hope in God.

Hence, doctor-assisted suicide would alter the ethos of our society. The world its advocates envision is a collection of autonomous individuals who make life-and-death decisions on the basis of their claim to be the sole owners of themselves. Theirs is a world of individuals who determine the worth of a life by appealing to some nebulous, subjective conception of personal happiness. Christian theology leads us to question whether this is the kind of society that honors God.

Viewing Life Through Theological Eyes

Perhaps no aspect of existence is of greater concern to us than our lives as individuals. Does theology say anything about this? Can we look at personal life through theological eyes? Not only can we, but we must. Being a disciple demands that I view myself through the lenses of Christian faith, a process that involves at least two crucial aspects.

First, viewing myself through theological eyes means understanding myself in accordance with the Christian belief system. It entails developing an unabashedly Christian sense of who I am. Theology, in other words, contributes to the formation of our personal identity. "Who am I?" is a perennial question, and determining personal identity is one of the significant challenges we all face, for we often do not know where to turn to discover who we are.

Lying in his bed, Charlie Brown is looking intently at the ceiling and musing to nobody in particular: "Sometimes I lie awake at night, and I ask, 'Why am I here?' Then a voice says, 'Where are you?' 'Here,' I say. 'Where is "here"?' says the voice. 'Wave your hand so I can see you.' " Turning on his side, the melancholy boy then sighs, "The nights are getting longer."

When we, like Charlie Brown, ask questions about our existence, such as "Who am I?" theological reflection points us toward the answers. Theology leads us to reaffirm the central aspects of our identity. It brings to our minds the biblical truths that should shape who we are, and it reminds us that the questions of personal identity can only be answered as we view ourselves within a theological context—as we define ourselves in accordance with God's defining of us. Theology reminds us that the central pillar of our identity lies in who we are as God's redeemed children. This—and nothing that anyone says—marks us as individuals. We are not God's children in isolation. Rather, we are God's as participants in a community of the redeemed. God is *our* heavenly Father.

With this solid foundation in place, theology leads us to consider "Who am I?" from another angle: "What is my ultimate purpose?" Our identity includes our God-given purpose for existence. God calls us to "be" in the world. And our being in the world has a purpose. Above all, this purpose is to bring glory to God as people who point toward the goal God has for creation. Bringing theology into life means viewing all that we are and do in the light of this overarching purpose. We ask ourselves how the various aspects of our lives fit into this goal.

"Who am I?" also involves "What is my calling within God's program?" While we all share this fundamental purpose for being, we each have an individual calling within it. God invites each of us to fulfill that purpose in a way that is uniquely ours. This unique manner includes the specific roles and responsibilities we have, such as family member, neighbor, citizen. It includes as well the specific vocation—employee, employer, homemaker, professional, student—into which God has placed us. Bringing theology into life means understanding ourselves as "vocational Christians," as disciples who serve God and advance God's program through our vocation.

Reflection on our identity quite naturally leads us to consider how we live out that identity in the midst of the day-to-day aspects of life. Thus viewing ourselves through theological eyes means, second, living in accordance with our fundamental convictions in the midst of the situations of life. In a word, bringing theology into life means living with integrity. Doing so requires that we understand what integrity means.

The standard dictionary definition of the term focuses on "uprightness in character" and traits such as honesty. True integrity, however, goes deeper. It has to do with authenticity. Persons of integrity are free from duplicity. With them, you don't go away wondering whether they are motivated by hidden agendas. Authenticity points us toward an even more important dimension. Integrity means "acting in accordance with one's stated beliefs." Persons of integrity stand for their convictions, even at great personal cost.

Thus "Christian integrity" means acting according to Christian belief, which is what discipleship is all about. Theology helps us to live with integrity by clarifying what belongs to Christian belief so that we can better explore the implications of our convictions for our lives. Theology reminds us that God and God's actions in the world provide the foundation for understanding the life of integrity. Specifically, Christian integrity involves living in such a way that our lives mirror God's own nature. The person of integrity is one whose conduct shows forth what God is like. Or as someone put it, "A Christian is someone whose life makes it easier to believe in God." Good theology fosters this in us.

9

An Invitation to Engage in Theology

*L*ucy and Linus are staring out the picture window watching rain pour from the sky. With a worried look on her face, Lucy remarks, "Boy, look at it rain. What if it floods the whole world?"

Linus replies confidently, "It will never do that. In the ninth chapter of Genesis, God promised Noah that would never happen again, and the sign of the promise is the rainbow."

Lucy looks relieved. "You've taken a great load off my mind."

"Sound theology has a way of doing that!" Linus responds matter-of-factly.

Indeed, sound theology does have a way of meeting the need of the moment! We began this book about theology with the affirmation that you already are a theologian—whether you know it or not. Of course, as we continued to explain, not everyone is a theologian in the same way. Linus told Lucy that "sound theology" has a way of taking a great load off people's minds. Our book has not been about developing just any theology, but sound theology. Only sound theology, whether engaged in by laypersons, pastors or professional theologians, truly aids in discipleship.

Again, you do not have to become a professional theologian or even an ordained minister to engage in sound theology. The tools and skills generally made available through a formal education are helpful in engaging in high-level critical and constructive theology, but these are not absolutely necessary to attaining a level of reflective thinking that will enhance your Christian discipleship.

If your goal is to become a pastor or professional theologian, you no doubt plan to attend Bible college, seminary or graduate school. The path toward becoming a theologian will open up before you in this manner. But what if you do not plan to take further coursework in biblical and theological studies? What if your only introduction to the study of theology is the course you are presently taking or just this book? We invite you to set out on a journey toward becoming a reflective lay Christian theologian anyway. In this chapter we will explain how to begin and continue for a lifetime on that pathway.

What Is Necessary for Being a Theologian?

As with any other avocation, engaging in lay theology requires some basic commitments and fundamental attitudes. Authentic Christianity will always incline a person toward those commitments and attitudes necessary to becoming a theologian. It is unlikely that these could be totally absent in any person who truly has a heart for God.

First, being a Christian theologian at any level requires that a person be more interested in knowing God than in amassing ideas about God. Dutch theologian Hendrikus Berkhof has commented that the lowest reaches of hell are reserved for theologians who are more interested in their own thoughts about God than in God himself! The first and most basic prerequisite to being a theologian at any level, then, is *a heart for God.*

Perhaps, though, you find yourself in that position of being keenly interested in ideas about God—say, questions of philosophical theology—without having a deep love for God. We invite you to stop immediately and begin to get to know God personally. Open your life to God through devotional reading of Scripture, through worship with a local community of Christians, and through prayer to God through his Son Jesus in the power of the Holy Spirit.

Only when you have truly encountered God and allowed God's Spirit to transform you—including renewing your mind—will the deeper and higher dimensions of theology open up to you. Before and apart from that, theology will always remain mere intellectual activity rather than life-transforming wisdom. At the same time, Christians who have even a minimal love for God will discover that the study of theology can deepen this love.

Second, being a theologian requires that you become dissatisfied with your present level of understanding. You must desire to deepen your comprehension of the Christian faith and be committed to growing toward mature thinking about God, yourself and the world. This dissatisfaction includes a healthy discontent with folk theology—the all-too-common patchwork of unexamined clichés, slogans, stories and half-baked notions about God that forms the thinking of many Christians today. And you must find unsatisfying the possibility of remaining at the level of accepting by sheer blind faith whatever you have been taught by your own Christian subculture. You must have such a strong desire to grow in a deepened faith that you are willing to question widely propagated yet questionable ideas and beliefs in the light of the gospel.

I (Roger) was spiritually nurtured in a small Christian denomination that tended to revel in what we have called folk theology. I thank God for the wonderful experiences I had at that denomination's summer youth camp and through its youth music and Bible quizzing programs. The evangelists who came to my home church were for the most part exemplary men and women who exuded love for God and encouraged strong Christian commitment. I will never regret being raised in that spiritually stimulating atmosphere. It was there that I learned to love Jesus Christ and the Bible.

However, the very Christianity instilled in me by these spiritual mentors contained seeds of reflection that grew into a hunger and thirst for more than the simple, unreflective piety of the people around me. I often hesitantly asked evangelists and pastors for answers to troubling intellectual questions about our faith. I was told that rather than question so much, I should remain content with what I now recognize as folk theology. These dear leaders had no books of Christian scholarship to give, no satisfying answers to offer, no genuine words of encouragement for me in my desire to find answers to satisfy the mind as well as the heart.

Out of desperation to know and understand—a desperation born of spiritual excitement, not doubt or skepticism—I eventually began moving away from the denomination of my upbringing. It had taught me to love God's Word, but it was unable to instruct me as to how to understand and apply it in the world of which I was a part. I had to throw out folk theology and blind faith in order to discover a greater, stronger conviction about truth that adds intellectual understanding and mental assent to heart experience. In the process, I discovered that head and heart are not necessarily antithetical.

As I left, I sadly noticed that because many of my friends and spiritual mentors in that denomination never found the courage to question, they ended up settling for borrowed beliefs. They had a theology that they accepted unquestioningly but that was not integrated into their own lives in contemporary society and culture. Unfortunately, those beliefs often are a distortion of true Christianity. Such theology is untranslatable to a world hungry for Christian answers to life's pressing problems, and it is based more on wishful thinking and pious feelings than on the gospel contained in God's Word.

Thus engaging in theology requires that you be dissatisfied with blind faith in other people's answers—so much so that you are willing to set out on the risky but exciting path of finding answers that are truly satisfying to the mind as well as to the heart.

Third, becoming a theologian requires that you be willing to work. Theology is not easy. Indeed, as with any endeavor undertaken with a goal of enrichment, "no pain, no gain!" Not only will engagement in theology sometimes lead you to leave behind comfortable but inadequate answers, it will also lead you through challenging reading, thinking and application. The result will be a stronger faith and a more effective life of discipleship.

The Risks and Rewards

The main reward you will receive from engaging in theology is an enriched and enhanced Christian life. A persistent and profoundly disturbing myth of much American Christianity is that to be an authentic Christian, a person must sacrifice the intellect. This widely held idea is wrong! Jesus said, "Love the Lord your God with all your heart and with all your soul and with all your mind" (Mt 22:37). We cannot love God with our minds if being a disciple entails sacrificing the intellect. Loving God with our minds includes putting all our intellectual abilities into our Lord's service. Theology—reflective Christianity—is one way of worshiping God with our minds. God wants us to think thoughts pleasing to him, and this includes knowing God as God is—to the best of our limited human capacities. God is not glorified by lazy or sloppy thinking.

A second reward of engaging in theology is finding answers to questions that arise in the course of living the Christian life in contemporary culture. Any person seeking to live as a disciple of Jesus Christ in today's world will encounter questions. These range from "Why doesn't God stop all the evil going on in the world?" to "How can God be 'three' and 'one' at the same time?" and "Is reincarnation compatible with Christianity?"

Theology is not so much a set of pat answers to these and other similar questions as it is a way of thinking toward answers. The only alternative to honestly seeking answers is refusing to live Christianly in public and thus refusing to engage in discussions with questioning seekers. This alternative is hardly compatible with authentic Christianity!

A third reward of theological engagement is having a belief system to fall back on during those inevitable periods of spiritual dryness when we cannot feel God's presence. I (Roger) will never forget my seminary theology professor's testimony about theology's sustaining power during his wife's long and losing battle with cancer. In the privacy of his office a few weeks after his wife died, this professor shared with me how he felt so numb that much of the time he couldn't sense God's presence. But 'hen he added that in spite of the absence of *feeling,* he still knew God was present, sustaining and supporting him. He knew this because of years of studying Scripture and developing a strong body of sound beliefs. For him, as for many others, theology became a medium—a sacrament, so to speak—of God's gracious power to sustain and strengthen when all capacity for feeling God had temporarily dried up.

Opposite rewards, theology does have risks. One risk of theologizing is the danger of substitution—substituting intellectualism for heartfelt faith. Every Christian who has followed the path of theology very far has heard stories of or has met people who were once deeply committed Christians but then traded a heart rich toward God for a "head trip." That is, they succumbed to the temptation to substitute reading books about the biblical witness for reading the witness itself. Or they allowed themselves to substitute concepts about God for knowing the living God who was present in their life.

This situation is similar to the person who began studying maps (cartography) because she loved to travel, but ended up confusing cartography with seeing the world. The risk of substitution is present in any intellectual endeavor. There is always the danger of moving so far into the study of something that we lose the original purpose for that study.

There are some safeguards that can help you avoid the danger of substitution. As you set out on the path of reflective Christianity, be sure to maintain strong ties with a local body of Christian believers through regular worship, Bible study and prayer. Also make certain that your personal prayer and devotional life grows along with your intellectual capacity for wrestling with the tough tasks of theology.

Depending on your denomination, a second risk you might face in theologizing is the potential loss of your current church affiliation. Some budding theologians quickly become persuaded that certain traditional formulations of Christian belief are simply wrong and therefore that they need to leave their church, their denomination or even Christianity itself. The risk of this last step—apostasy—is not inherent to theology. It can become a danger only when a theologian gets sidetracked from faithful reflection rooted in a strong personal faith in God's Word.

However, all theologizing that goes beyond folk theology carries with it the risk of discovering doctrinal problems—even dogmatic flaws—in one's own church or denomination. You must be prepared for such discoveries. And be advised that honest reflection on the biblical message could even necessitate your moving out of a church or denominational tradition if you come to see it as having wandered from sound Christian teaching.

A final risk is that of being misunderstood. Even if you tread the path of reflective Christianity lightly and cautiously, you will probably find some people pulling away from you—especially if your religious context is heavily influenced by folk theology. Some believers will not be able to understand your desire to grow intellectually in your faith.

I (Roger) will never forget a family reunion held the day before I left for theological study in Germany. A concerned but misguided uncle pulled me aside and expressed his fear that so much study of theology would destroy both my faith and common sense. His parting words to me were "Remember, there is such a thing as an overeducated idiot."

You may need to be prepared to hear comments such as these, even if you do not undertake years of formal theological education. Some well-meaning Christians may feel threatened by your new acumen and may distance themselves from it—from you—to protect their comfortable folk theology.

The risks of engaging in theology may sound frightening, but the rewards outweigh the risks if you launch and then continue your pursuit of theological understanding in a spirit of humble submission to God's Word and the Holy Spirit.

Becoming a Reflective Christian

So what if you have decided to pursue the goal of becoming a reflective lay Christian? What if you feel the pull toward one day pursuing formal study of theology and want to start developing a theological mind now? In either case, there are some basic tools and skills you should begin acquiring.

Perhaps you are reading this book as part of an introductory course in theology. In that case, you are already engaging in the process of developing theological acumen. During the course you will no doubt acquire additional skills. If, however, you are reading this book on your own, you too can begin collecting or making use of certain important resources.

Earlier we explained that theology has three main tools: the biblical message, the theological heritage of the church and contemporary culture. Theology attempts to bring all three together interdependently. Therefore, your first step is to become aware of these sources of theology and to put them to use.

Take the Bible first. Do you have access to a library containing Bible aids and helps such as introductions to biblical books, commentaries, word studies, concordances and Bible dictionaries? If not, you may need to purchase some basic printed helps. If a theological library is readily at hand, find out where these important resources for Bible study are and become familiar with them. Some of the basic resources for making good use of your Bible in developing your theological mind include

☐ a good study Bible in a recent translation such as the New International Version

☐ a recent one-volume Bible commentary

☐ a Bible dictionary or encyclopedia

☐ a concordance and/or topical Bible keyed to your Bible translation

In addition, begin a program of serious Bible study alternating between major books of the two testaments. For example, read and study Paul's epistle to the Romans using a good evangelical commentary.[1] When you run into an interpretation or perspective in your commentary that interests or concerns you, study that concept using the Bible dictionary, cross-references in your study Bible and other study helps. Keep a journal of your discoveries and thoughts as you study. After finishing Romans, turn to Isaiah in the Old Testament. Then alternate back and forth from the New to the Old.

Another way to use these resources for theological study of the Bible is to focus on a particular doctrine or concept and use a topical Bible or concordance to trace it throughout Scripture. Use the commentary and dictionary as you arrive at key passages that form the basis for that concept. For example, begin with the concept of "divine revelation." Use the tools and resources to study all the major passages that deal with God's self-disclosure. Keep a journal to record your discoveries and thoughts.

Second, you should also familiarize yourself with historical theology—the theological heritage of the Christian churches. Basic resources for doing so include the following:

☐ a dictionary or encyclopedia of church history or history of theology

☐ a recent one-volume summary of church history or historical theology

☐ a volume containing the major creeds and confessions of faith of various churches

☐ a copy of your own church's or denomination's statement of faith

The best way to proceed is to read the one-volume summary of church history or historical theology and use the other tools to study in more depth specific concepts, movements or developments that catch your attention as you read about the church's heritage of theology. Be sure to familiarize yourself with your own church's theological heritage as well as the biblical and historical background to its basic beliefs.

Third, study your own cultural context. Begin a program of paying attention to the messages propagated by various media. Be attuned to happenings in popular culture (music, literature, plays and so on), follow political developments and become aware of the interactions between religious movements and secular culture.

Helpful resources for the task of studying the culture you are part of would include

☐ a weekly news magazine

☐ television

☐ a daily newspaper, the radio, the Internet or computer online services

☐ courses at a local community college or other institution of higher learning

In addition, several Christian periodicals specialize in analyzing culture from a Christian perspective. Obtain one or two of these through your local library, or subscribe to them yourself.

Your study of these resources is a lifelong journey. As you embark on that journey, carry out theological projects from time to time. For instance, suppose you overhear someone mention "the social gospel" derogatorily. As a budding theologian, you should find your curiosity piqued. You may ask, "What is the social gospel?" Carry out a research project—read dictionary articles, chapters in books, magazine articles and so on—with an eye to first understanding and then evaluating for yourself this phenomenon in American church history. A good place to start would be a readers' index at a library. Ask a reference librarian to help you find articles on the social gospel in periodicals or anthologies.

Do the same with a variety of concepts, doctrines, movements and people. If you are unsure where to begin or what to undertake, start with your own church's founder(s). Where did your denomination originate? Why did it begin? What theological impulses shaped its beginnings? What about today? How does its theological orientation compare with those of other Christian traditions? Your own church library would probably be of help in this study.

At some point in this process you will be ready to pick up a book of systematic theology and begin reading it. Ask your pastor to recommend one, or browse through a seminary or Christian college library or bookstore. There are literally hundreds available in all sizes and from every conceivable denominational perspective.

All of the methods mentioned above have to do with gathering knowledge you may need in becoming theologically reflective. In the process of becoming knowledgeable you will begin to expand your mind. You will be amazed at how many times you come across a certain idea or issue once you have become aware of it. Your new-found knowledge will also help your mind focus on religious issues in the church and in the world around you. Don't settle for simply becoming theologically literate, however. Make every attempt to begin reflecting on your experience of the church and the world in the light of the knowledge you are gaining.

For example, instead of simply singing hymns and choruses in church by rote, examine and analyze the words for their theological messages, being careful not to become overly critical. Ask yourself, *Do I really believe what I am singing? Are the words and the message compatible with the gospel? What aspect of Christianity's theological heritage do they express? Do they speak to contemporary culture?* Then you might think about the music itself: *Is it an appropriate vehicle for expressing the mood of the hymn or song? Do the words and music fit together?*

Beyond gaining knowledge and practicing critical reflection, there is no more effective way to learn than to teach. In other words, if you want to grow in your own theological abilities, you should try teaching someone else. Teaching will force you to study and think. In addition, your mind will retain information and grasp concepts much more efficiently if you are expressing what you are learning. Volunteer to teach a Sunday-school class or Bible study group at your church. Lead a small group or start a home Bible study. Or offer to start and lead a Bible study within the framework of a parachurch organization such as Youth for Christ or Bible Study Fellowship.

You might be wondering, *At what point in this process will I become a theologian?* Recall a key theme we have been trying to drive home throughout this entire book: *you already are a theologian!* Your goal is not to become a theologian, but to strive to enhance your theological acumen and skills through a process of becoming familiar with theology's sources and tools and by exercising your reflective abilities.

Thinking Critically and Constructively

Perhaps the largest hurdle or greatest chasm between the merely knowledgeable lay Christian thinker and the truly reflective lay theologian is the ability to think about Christian truth critically and constructively. Moving beyond the level of knowledge to the higher level of reflective thinking is important. But how may that happen, since there is no simple set of steps from "literate" to "reflective"? Some exercises that have to do with perceiving relationships between or among ideas will help you make that transition.

First, keep a journal of your thoughts—not just facts—about your Christian beliefs. Which ones would you die for? Why? Which ones would you argue for but not die for? Why? Which ones would you be willing to throw aside or radically revise at the first serious challenge? Why? This exercise will help you see the shades of importance among various beliefs and expand your mind's ability to recognize reasons for beliefs.

If you would like to try this exercise but don't know where to begin, start with your own church's or denomination's statement of faith.

Study it with an eye toward determining what among the beliefs stated there are the essentials and the nonessentials. Use it as the basis for the journaling exercise.

Perhaps the most critical aspect of this exercise—and the most difficult to guide—is answering the "Why?" questions. As you concentrate on which beliefs are essential and which are not, begin to reflect on the criteria you are using. Are you applying merely subjective tests, such as what beliefs you find comfortable or familiar? Or are your criteria more objective? That is, are you evaluating beliefs on the basis of their connection to the biblical message—the gospel itself, the theological heritage of Christianity and their ability to speak to people today? Various criteria may have a proper place, but the more sophisticated levels of theological reflection rely on the latter (the objective) more than the former (the subjective).

You probably recognize that the exercise just described is closely linked to the critical task of theology—especially its role in categorizing beliefs. Now we will suggest an exercise for increasing reflective ability in carrying out for yourself an aspect of theology's constructive task. Thinking back to the role of integrative motif as outlined in chapter seven, ask yourself, *What integrative motif brings coherence to my Christian beliefs?*

You probably do operate as if one particular concept about God, yourself and the world forms a hub that stands at the center and holds together the spokes of the wheel of your theology. Through a process of reflection, attempt to discover what it is. For some Christians the faith revolves around the theme of God's love. For others it is God's sovereignty or majesty. For yet others it is the future (eschatology), or creation or covenant. Earlier we advocated community as a viable contemporary integrative motif. Whether or not you are able to decide what your present integrative motif is, set out on a journey to discover what it should be. Ask yourself, *What single theme holds all the diverse strands of biblical Christianity together?* That is, where do all the beliefs you hold meet? What one theme is so crucial and comprehensive that without it everything else would fall apart?

Again, it would help to keep a journal of your thoughts about this as they develop. Try out different candidates for the job of integrative motif, and see if they hold up under scrutiny. Of all the possibilities, which one seems to include within itself everything else so that all else unfolds from it?

Much of what we have suggested in these exercises relates to developing a synoptic vision of the biblical message, the theological heritage of the church and contemporary culture. A synoptic vision is a holistic perspective that attempts to draw into coherence the otherwise blooming, buzzing confusion of data. This is a fairly high level of reflection. It requires a degree of familiarity with the data (for example, of the sources of theology) plus an ability to recognize connections, patterns and shades of importance. The exercises we have suggested—and others you may come up with on your own—are aimed at helping you develop this level of reflection. The process will not happen overnight, but as you work at it you will gain the ability to develop a synoptic vision.

One final note: Do not try to engage in theological reflection alone. Converse with other concerned Christians and leaders about your discoveries. We learn from each other. And others can caution us away from potentially dangerous paths.

Whether or not you actually carry out the formal exercises outlined above, you can move toward becoming a reflective Christian lay theologian. More important than any exercises is a commitment and determination to grow and mature in thinking through your Christian faith within a community of God's people and in relation to your cultural context. If you choose to do this, you will inevitably become more effective as "salt" and "light" in the world where God has placed you.

So—Who Needs Theology?

Lucy follows Linus around the house, pointing at him and shouting, "You *have* to give me a Christmas present! It says so in the Bible!"

Undisturbed, Linus sits in an armchair looking into a book: "You're bluffing. . . . The Bible says nothing about giving Christmas presents!" Lucy looks nonplussed. "It doesn't?" she asks.

As she sighs, Linus declares in a self-satisfied way, "You can't bluff an old theologian!"

We have attempted to demonstrate and explain the many needs for and contributions of theology. We hope that you now agree that theology is of more value than simply pointing out other people's mistakes! Theology is crucial to the entire task of living Christianly in both church and world. Living involves questioning. Living Christianly involves asking and attempting to answer questions about God and the world. Thus living Christianly involves theology.

We hope you will embark on a lifelong journey of theological discovery, with the goal of enhancing and enriching your own life of discipleship as well as the strength and influence of the church of Jesus Christ.

Notes

Introduction
[1]*Christianity Today,* October 24, 1994, p. 75.

Chapter 2: Not All Theologies Are Equal
[1]John Updike, *Roger's Version* (New York: Ballantine Books, 1986).

Chapter 3: Defining Theology
[1]Sidney I. Landau, ed., *The Doubleday Dictionary for Home, School and Office* (Garden City, N.Y.: Doubleday, 1975), p. 763.
[2]"Grace and Grit," *Vancouver Sun TV Times,* March 31, 1995, p. 4.

Chapter 4: Defending Theology
[1]Some doubt exists about the precise reasons for these stipulations in Bethany College's charter. It may be that the founder included the prohibition of a chair of theology in perpetuity to avoid church-state conflicts. This seems questionable, however, in that the college is private and not public, and since the Bible was to be its main textbook.
[2]English translation by John Knox Press, 1965.

Chapter 5: Theology's Tasks and Traditions
[1]We are grateful to our friend and Roger's colleague, retired theology professor Alfred Glenn, for this illustration of theology's constructive task.

[2]H. Richard Niebuhr, *The Kingdom of God in America* (New York: Harper & Row, 1959), p. 193.

Chapter 7: Constructing Theology in Context

[1]Philip Bliss, "Let the Lower Lights Be Burning."

[2]Note that we are not suggesting that community is the only possible central theme for your systematic theology. We offer it here only as an example of an integrative motif that we have found useful.

Chapter 9: An Invitation to Engage in Theology

[1]For example: John Stott, *Romans: God's Good News for the World* (Downers Grove, Ill.: InterVarsity Press, 1994).